Great Men and Praying Women

A young Muslim man finds Jesus and a new respect for women.

Dr. Ghazanfar Abdullah, MD, FAAC

About the cover

God sees both partners of a marriage as equals, just as it is hard to distinguish the male from the female in this pair of lovebirds. There is equality, but male and female are not the same, as each has a specific role which is complementary to the role of the other. Husband and wife can do great and mighty things to advance the kingdom of God, as long as they do not let Satan put a wedge between them, and the couple stays under the protection and guidance of God's Holy Spirit. Such as the scene when lovebirds kiss in a Heavenly garden.

Copyright © 2022 **But for God Publishing**

All rights reserved. No part of this publication may be reproduced, distributed, or transmitted in any form or by any means, including photocopying, recording, or other electronic or mechanical methods, without the prior written permission of the publisher, except in the case of brief quotations embodied in critical reviews and certain other noncommercial uses permitted by copyright law. For permission requests, write to the publisher, addressed "Attention: Book Rights and Permission," at the address below.

Published in the United States of America

ISBN 978-1-959173-35-9 (SC)

But for God Publishing
1 Deer Park Road
Orangeburg NY State 10962
gzabdullah@yahoo.com

Ordering Information and Rights Permission:

Quantity sales. Special discounts might be available on quantity purchases by corporations, associations, and others. For details, contact the publisher at the address above.

For Book Rights Adaptation and other Rights Permission. Call us at toll-free 1-888-945-8513 or send us an email at admin@stellarliteray.com.

Table of Contents

About the cover: ii
Introduction: 1
   The Taliban Should Love and Honor their Wives. 1
   Belonging to the Ghetto. 8
Chapter 1: Suffering for Christ. 14
   The Wooden Cross 14
   The Contrast between Suffering for Christ, versus Suffering for our Addictions. . 16
   Pick up your Cross and Follow Jesus. 19
Chapter2: Suffering through Marriage. 22
   The Vine, the Gardener, and the Pruning Shears (my wife's elbows). 25
   Shaken, Not Stirred. 29
   Thirty-five years and counting! Letter to my wife and soulmate 35
Chapter 3: Love is the Glue. 36
   Jesus too was a carpenter. 37
   Heart Space for Love. 40
   Love, Power, and Soundness of Mind. 44
Chapter 4: Faith. 47
   Faith Like A Child. 47
   Questioning God versus Being Quiet Before God. 53
   The Parable of the Screen Door. 55
Chapter 5: The Holy Spirit. 58
   His Grandpa's Shirt 60
   Jesus's First Miracle, and my Folly. 64
Chapter 6: Courtship and Understanding Women. 67
   The Parable of Peristalsis. 69
   The Parable of the Pedestal. 70
   The Marriage Bed 72
      Part 1: God's Love, God's Hierarchy, and Our Submission---- Somebody Tell a Feminist that Submission is Not a Dirty Word. 74
      Part 2: The Biblical Rules for Sex----Rules of the Road for the 'Highway of Life.' 84

- Part 3: How can we make the Viagra man a Better Listener? 92
- Chapter 7: Raising Children. 102
  - The Arrow and the Bow. 102
  - From boys 2 men (a famous boy band), 2 priests of the home. 104
  - Polygamy versus monogamy. 107
  - Erection versus Enlightenment. 109
  - Ambition versus contentment. 113
  - Ode to a Young Man. 115
- Chapter 8: Growing Old Gracefully. 116
  - Trouble. 116
  - Grandpa Loves to Putter. 118
  - Generations 124
  - My Friend, The Bully: How My Meek Father Inherited The World. 128
  - How I Expanded As I Shrank 133
  - Preparing for eternity. 135
  - God is love 136
  - The Sinner's Prayer. 137
- Chapter 9: Understanding Muslims. 138
  - What would Jesus do with Muslims? (WWJDWM). 138
  - Don't have a Cow Man! Better Atone your Sins with the Blood of Jesus. 142
  - We have lost our First Love. 143
  - God gently calls us, but the word of God is a double edged sword. 145
- Chapter 10: Ten texts, Difficult Questions, Life Changing Answers. 146
  - Excerpts from the book: Great Men and Praying Women 146
- Biography: 159

Introduction:

The Taliban Should Love and Honor their Wives.

August 15, 2021, the Taliban had just taken over Afghanistan. A female CNN news reporter was interviewing three high-ranking Taliban generals. She was wondering if anything had changed after 20 years of American occupation. She asked, "Will the new Afghanistan be a democracy, with fair elections for your leadership?"

The desert sands were being whipped up by the wind while she eagerly waited for an answer. The most elder of the three Taliban generals was leaning on his American made machine gun. He quickly and decisively answered, "yes, the Taliban will have democratic elections, we will fight global warming, and we seek to be a part of the international community."

The CNN reporter seemed a little surprised, but very pleased, at his answer. Tufts of blonde hair were peeking out from under her head dress, and then she asked a probing follow up question, "what kind of rights will women have in the new Afghanistan?"

The Taliban general responded in a matter-of-fact tone, saying, "women will be treated fairly under the Islamic sharia law."

The CNN reporter was beginning to feel her oats. Maybe she could single-handedly get the Taliban to cower to western values, convert to Christianity, and believe the virtues of woke feminism. She had the general's undivided attention and the camera was rolling. The next question that she was going to ask was going to make her famous, and perhaps CNN would regain some of it's long lost gravitas.

Her blue eyes were batting expectantly, as she asked, "so, in this democratic country of Afghanistan, where your elections are fair, when do you envision having a female leader of your country?"

All of a sudden, the gray bearded general looked confused. He asked the interpreter to repeat the reporter's question. He looked at his comrade to the left, and his comrade to the right, and then he burst out laughing, "Stop filming! Stop filming!"

The man on the left of him was holding his belly as he laughed. The man on the right slapped the elderly Taliban general on the back as he almost fell over laughing, while he begged the cameraman, "stop filming! Stop filming!"

The CNN reporter never got her answer, but then again, maybe she did. Still fake news.

On another interview, this one is fictional (a la Sacha Baron Cohen's movie, "Borat"), some high-ranking Taliban leader, named Borat, was confronted by a reporter who pointed out that "fifty percent of the population is women, so why don't they get an equal say in the matters of the Afghani government?"

First, Borat stroked his beard, as if to reap wisdom from it, and then he methodically answered, "numerically, women are fifty percent of the population, but the opinion of each individual woman is worth only one quarter of that of a man."

General Borat continued, "the woman has a brain size like that of a squirrel. This is why if a woman claims she is the victim of rape, she would need four male witnesses to collaborate her story; otherwise, the judge would throw out her case.

Borat continued, "so if four guys want to rape a woman on a particular night, one of them will have to sit out, to keep the others safe from legal retribution."

What's this obsession with the number four? Thirty-five years ago, back in the good old US of A, the girlfriend who would eventually become my wife asked me, "am I just the first of three, or four, other women who you're going to marry at the same time as me?"

I was a Muslim back then, I am a Christian now, but back then I knew I had to say something to keep my girlfriend believing in our relationship. I said, "one woman is like having one hole in my head, in Islam were allowed to have four wives, which would be equivalent to having four holes in my head. Why would I want my brains to leak out four times as fast?"

I thought I was being romantic and clever! Boy, did I have a lot to learn. Thirty-five years later I'm still married to that girl who I met in the emergency room of Lincoln hospital, in the Bronx, New York City. And although she has the divorce lawyer's number on speed dial, I have learned how to love my wife as Christ loved the church. I put her on a high and heavy pedestal, which I designed so she could not easily lift it up, and throw at me, in a fit of anger.

My friend, Adam **Elsayed**, a 27-year-old pharmaceutical representative who calls on my office, wasn't as lucky as me. His father, a Muslim, left his family to start another family, when Adam was only 10 years old. Adam had to learn to play catch by himself. He would throw the ball high in the air, and he would positioned his baseball mitt so he would catch the ball before it hit the ground. He was an avid reader, but no one ever read him a bedtime story. He was a sharp dresser, but no one ever taught him how to make a knot for his tie. Thankfully, his father wasn't around to give him advice on how to raise multiple polygamous families.

His father would disappear for weeks and months at a time, "for business," until he eventually divorced his first wife to pursue the next wife. Adam might have never come to know about his step brothers and sisters, were it not that his father developed cancer and thought it was prudent to have Adam look after his younger step siblings, in the event of the father's death.

"Not cool!" That was Adam's initial response when he found out that for the last seventeen years he had been cheated out of having a father. To make matters worse, several of his aunts and uncles, who fully knew about the polygamous family, kept it secret from Adam. When Adam confronted them, they said, "well, in Islam what your father was doing was completely right, he could've even had two more wives if he wanted."

Adam came to know about his father's parallel family only about a year before I met him. "Not in America! This should never happen in America," Adam opined to me when he shared with me his frustration. I could feel his pain. But in a strange sense we needed each other: he needed a father figure, and I could always use another son. I have two biological sons, a daughter, and six grandchildren, but I always welcome having another spiritual son, or daughter. Incidentally, I have a son also named Adam, and my father's name is Syed——my adopted son's name is Adam Elsayed. Coincidence? I think not, this is God's proof that we are family. My own children are spoiled, they don't need my advice, or read the books that I've written, but Adam was different. He was searching for something more than what Islam and his biological father had to offer. He was seeking God, and I was the instrument that God provided for his help. I became Adam's spiritual father and he became my spiritual son.

I know firsthand that spiritual bonds can be stronger then biological roots. Twenty-two years ago, when I first became a Christian, facing persecution from my parents and other relatives, I cried out to the Lord to help me reconcile with my family. As I prayed, there was a sudden peace that washed over my aching heart. I had a moment of extreme clarity, as the Lord brought me peace through a soft, still voice, which said, "I am your family! And the sisters and brothers you have in the church are your real sisters and brothers. They are your family as well."

From that point on, when it came to the approval of my Muslim relatives, I could take it or leave it. This realization has given me peace, confidence, and self-esteem. I want to share this peace that I got from the Lord with my friend and spiritual son, Adam **Elsayed**.

I want to share with Adam this peace that goes beyond understanding. I want to mentor my adopted son, my disciple, so that he can have all the guidance that he needs to advance his spiritual life in a world that is chaotic, and confusing. Just look at what is going on in Afghanistan.

The Taliban cannot be conquered, the Russians tried, the Americans tried, let's see now if the Chinese try. One of the Taliban's favorite sayings about the 20 year American occupation is this, "the Americans have the clocks, but the Taliban have the time." That may be true, but God has the time, the grace, the mercy, the love, and the forgiveness. God is not moved by waving machine guns, or by merciless executions, falsely done in God's name. This makes God grieve.

Now that the American occupation is over, let's see how the Taliban will govern; particularly, with regard to how they treat women. Twenty years feels more like sixty years for a population whose life-expectancy is only thirty years. American millennials start "Adulting" at age thirty. For a whole generation the Taliban women experienced democracy, freedom, the Internet, education, jobs, and pop culture. But some women and girls may have experienced something much more powerful then Western freedom; many of them have experienced the freedom that can only be found through a relationship with Jesus Christ. Humility, submission, obedience—— these are components of fervent prayer but, sadly, Afghani women have practiced these traits while being oppressed by Afghani men.

God listens attentively to the prayers of mothers, daughters, sisters, and all women. Taliban men should recognize the power of a woman's prayer, and they should put that prayer to work to rebuild their nation. The saying goes, "behind every great man is a great woman." But I say, "a tough woman, who is honored and listened to by her man, builds a great family, and yes, she inculcates a Godly purpose in her man." Hence they become great men and praying women.

In my life, God picked the perfect soulmate for me. As you read this book, you will see, my wife was a hard wife for me to deal with, but I loved, honored, and respected her, and she helped me grow in every aspect of my life. She helped me succeed, but more importantly, she helped me avoid a lot of boneheaded mistakes that could have gotten me killed, or at least in jail. When I was young, with a high testosterone level, I thought I was superman! I'm not just bashing men here. Let's not deny that estrogen causes a lot of unnecessary anxiety, depression, and gossip. But how do we coexist with the opposite sex? How can Arabs and Jews coexist? This book has the answer to all conflicts. I will give you a hint. His name is Jesus!

Coming from a Muslim background, my instinct was to steam roller my wife, and hate a Jew—— I was a Taliban wanna be. But my wife wasn't having any of it. Women give good advice, and it often balances the arrogant, testosterone driven goals that we men tend to set for ourselves.

There is a bumper sticker that reads, "real men ask for directions." Love for our wives should supersede the desire to 'mansplain' them. The best advice for the Taliban is that they should love their wives the way Christ loved the church, and he died for the church.

Grace is getting what you don't deserve, mercy is not getting what you do deserve, and God's power is made perfect in our weakness. Women are the weaker vessel, but they are attached to a powerful God, who listens to their prayers—— women should be loved, honored, and respected by men, because women's prayers connect men to an Almighty God.

The Taliban's macho arrogance has to die before Afghanistan can rise up and become a member of the international community. Instead of dishonoring their women, Taliban men would do well if they got in touch with the 'feminine traits' of prayer: humility, submission, obedience. Then maybe, God would shower Afghanistan with grace, mercy, forgiveness, and love. If the Taliban were to have a harmonious relationship with their women folk, this would go a long way to improve their relationship with God, and also their relationship with the international community.

Elsayed: I liked this introduction the most! "I am your family! And the sisters and brothers you have in the church are your real sisters and brothers. They are your family as well." This part is so important to me, and I remember you telling me just because someone isn't blood related to you, doesn't mean you can't have family ties with them, or be closer with them than your actual blood related family. Thanks for discipling me, and would you please tell the readers how you are going to format this book, as it relates to our text messages.

Abdullah: My four previous Christian books were written as a collection of essays, life-inspired and scripturally footnoted. Very boring. The format of this book, however, has a smattering of scripturally sound essays, within a backdrop of unedited text conversations between Adam Elsayed and myself. He asked some very good questions, and I did my best to give him practical, sometimes hilarious answers. Fortunately, we both share a great sense of humor.

School is open and we have a classroom without walls. You don't need a COVID mask, or a COVID vaccine. Not even the teacher's union can shut us down for political gain. My clinic, in the South Bronx of New York City, is really just a church, cleverly disguised as a clinic.

Bring to this school/clinic/church your weak and your sick, your smart and your strong, and even your trespassers, because all are welcome. But don't be biased, or opinionated. Just leave your swords, guns, and your suicide vests at the door, please. I already have a crew cut, I don't need one of those really short Taliban-style haircuts, from the neck up. I only lost my head once for my wife, and that was 35 years ago. She's still a knockout! And yes, my brains slowly leaked out through just one hole in my head. Now I have the brain size of a squirrel.

Elsayed: Why is the first essay of this book titled, 'Belonging to the Ghetto?'

Abdullah: It comforts me to know that Jesus Christ, himself, had a hard time ministering in his hometown. To the people of Bethlehem, Jesus would always just be the son of a carpenter. God adopted me into His family, and now I am trying to bring my extended family, the whole world, into God's family. I guess, that's what you call evangelism.

In the ghetto your very survival depends on being able to know what makes you and what breaks you, everything else is just noise. Spirituality is all that matters. If we are spiritually connected, through God's Holy Trinity, then it won't matter if we live in the sandy ghettos of Afghanistan, or the rainforests of Brazil, or the concrete jungle of the South Bronx——because wherever we are, God is here. God is always with us. Amen.

Belonging to the Ghetto.

Sometimes I find it hard to understand why I don't fit in. No one is listening.

I give wise counsel but no one takes heed, not my children.

I write spiritual books that no one reads, definitely not my wife.

The Muslims don't read my books because I'm Christian.

The Christians don't read my books because I'm Ghetto, so real, so raw.

But the Ghetto people read my books because they are searching for God.

I know what it's like to be "Ghetto," and to be disenfranchised.

As a Muslim I was kicked out of a mosque.

As a Christian I was kicked out of a worship team, a men's group, and even a church.

It's a long story, but it has nothing to do with my singing voice, my masculinity, or my love for Jesus. Why do I get into so much trouble?

I am Ghetto, and I don't fit into any particular religious community.

Jesus had a similar problem in his hometown, where he could not do miracles because his own people lacked faith.

They said, "was not this Jesus merely the carpenter's son, he's certainly not the son of God, but only the son of Mary and Joseph."

Jesus said, "only in his hometown, among his relatives, and in his own house, is a prophet without honor."

Back to my Ghetto story. I may be misunderstood, but I am loved, because Jesus went into the Ghetto looking for the one lost sheep. I was the one Jesus saved! I am loved by the unconditional, unconventional, and even desperate love of Jesus Christ!

As I have been loved unconditionally, so too can I love those who society finds unlovable. God created me for such a time as this. I am a doctor to the South Bronx.

My nagging wife, who is a nurse, tells me, "nothing you could do, or say, will ever impress me." Together we show compassion to HIV positive, substance abusing, mentally ill people of the Bronx. They have made some bad choices, but they are searching for God's love.

The Pharisees tried to trap Jesus in a lie, they asked him, "why do you go to places where there are tax collectors and prostitutes?"

Jesus gave back the perfect answer, he said, "does not a doctor go where the sick people are?"

I guess I'm in good company, because I'm a doctor in the Ghetto,

And the Master Physician——Jesus—— was Ghetto like me. Is that an insult? No. Jesus didn't fit into any religious norms, in fact he was rejected by the Jews.

The Bible describes Jesus as "the cornerstone that was rejected by the builders." In masonry terms, the cornerstone is the most important part of the foundation.

The cornerstone keeps the entire structure plumb and level, just as the sacrifice of Jesus is the foundation of the Christian faith.

Yet Jesus was disenfranchised, maligned, disgraced, beaten and abandoned; nevertheless, Jesus carried out the will of God, as he was nailed to the cross. The cross I carry has no nails. I can only hope to someday become the pinky-finger on the hand of God, as He uses me to heal my patients, and build their faith, in the Ghetto of the South Bronx.

Elsayed: It's great that you're doing God's work in the South Bronx, but how did you get to this point? What were the events and circumstances that led you here?

Abdullah: Before God could use me, He had to break my old spirit, and mold me a new one. God use my wife as a wrecking ball to destroy my old foundations. The Taliban don't listen to their wives, but I do. She weighs 100 pounds less than me but she's really, really tough.

When I first laid my eyes on her in the emergency room at Lincoln hospital, I said to myself "Allah has favored me," but after I became a Christian I look at the same woman, who is now my wife, and say, "the Lord is trying to whip me into shape!"

In 1960, I was born in Calcutta, India, into a Muslim family, and we moved to America in 1963. In 1985, I married a prayer-warrior from the Philippines. She was a Born-again Christian for only a year when she met me, prior to that she was Catholic, and she became a Muslim at my request when we were married; it took her another ten years for her to become an alpha-female, convert back to Christianity, and she prayed me into the Kingdom of God. For three weeks straight she would wake up at 3 AM and plead the blood of Jesus over my forehead.

When I became a Christian she was not surprised, but instead, she was expecting this miracle to happen.

In 1998 I converted to Christianity by the grace of God, and by the powerful prayers of my wife, and by Jesus who visited me in a dream while I was still a Muslim. The dream took place in a hospital conference room, where doctors get together to discuss difficult cases. There must have been 10,000 patient charts on the conference room table, and standing at the head of the table was none other than Jesus Christ.

In my dream, Jesus motioned me towards him, and he simply said, "bring them to me and I will heal them."

Jesus was talking about every patient that I would ever touch with my stethoscope. In the dream, I fell to my knees and burst out into tears. You don't see Jesus and stay haughty and standing. The very next morning, I recited the sinners prayer with my wife's Pastor, and my first pastor, Pastor Carl Johnson.

Elsayed: Is It true that Muslims tend to be visited by Jesus and dreams and visions? When you started seeing all these signs, and seeing Jesus in your dreams, were you closed off to Christianity? Were you still a devoted Muslim, or were you opened to the idea? Do you think these signs come to everyone?

Abdullah: Yes, absolutely true. Stubborn people in general, and Muslims specifically, need to see Jesus himself before they can let down their barriers and receive the gift of Jesus's love, which comes with the ultimate gift of reconciliation with God.

Jesus reveals himself to those who are seeking him, but are stubborn. Dreams and visions are not for those who are seeking but are not stubborn.

Even the Taliban, if they take a break from beating their wives, and were to seek God, then I am sure that they would have dreams and visions of Jesus. Problem: the Taliban are stubborn enough, but are they seeking God?

I'll pay you $1 million if you fly to Afghanistan and tell the Taliban that they "need to learn how to pray like a girl!"

Elsayed: Silly you! I'll be sure to be on the look out for dreams and visions! I'm definitely open to it! I'll stay **seeking and stubborn**.

Abdullah: I was a card-carrying, five times a day praying, on fire for Mohammad, Muslim. I was stubborn, but I was seeking.

The first sign I had was when a voice, in my carpentry workshop, that told me, "Jesus too was a carpenter." This incident happened seven years before I became a Christian. I even asked my wife, "was Jesus ever a Carpenter?"

She said, "yes, but why are you asking?"

I said, "no reason, no reason."

I didn't want her to know that I had a miraculous vision about Jesus.

Elsayed: how do you know you've found a good mentor? Where do you look for one?

Abdullah: God sends people into your life, as long as you are a seeker of God. For example, if God hadn't sent me into your life, then he would've sent someone else. The bottom line is that you were a seeker of God. The seeker never finds God, but God finds the seeker. It's like the story of the little boy who was lost in the mall. When the police finally reunited him with his mother he told the police, "my mommy was lost, it's a good thing you helped me find her."

The process starts from the inside out, not from the outside in. You don't find God, he finds you.

You take one step towards God, and He takes 100 steps towards you. It's like the parable of the one lost sheep. God comes looking for the one sheep that is lost, leaving the 99 sheep that are safely found. God is actively drawing us nearer to Him.

If you thirst for God, then he will thirst for you. As an old Islamic proverb says, "oh you who are thirsty for the tea, you don't realize that the tea is also thirsty for you. "

If you pray for guidance, and keep a pure heart and an open mind, then God will send you the right mentor. This will be in addition to your internal mentor, which is the Holy Spirit, who dwells in every believer's heart.

Elsayed: Any other miraculous example?

Abdullah: Yes, a negative one. Two years before I became a Christian I was watching CNN, before it became fake news. CNN was covering the 'million man march' in Washington, DC.

I watched as Christian men of all races were praying to God in little circles. They were holding hands and praying fervently, with their eyes closed. The sight of this on television really moved me. I wanted to be one of those men, but then a vicious voice, a fiery-dart from Satin, entered my mind. It's sad, "you could never be one of those men, you are not a Christian. You are a Muslim for life."

And so I had to wait two more years before I became a Christian. That's what I get for watching CNN. It was still fake news back then.

Elsayed: Any other miraculous example?

Abdullah: Yes. When I first became a Christian, I had a lot to learn about women. At the instruction of a pastor, I did a one person communion with God. After I had a small sip of wine and a bite of a cracker, I asked God to show me what I needed to learn, I did this by randomly twice opening up the Bible, and these two scriptures (below) jumped out at me. The first scripture confirmed for me that the woman is the weaker vessel, the second scripture told me that God's power is made perfect in weakness, the upshot of all this: women may be weak but they are attached to a powerful God. And they are not to be messed with!

1 Peter 3:7 NIV

[7] Husbands, in the same way be considerate as you live with your wives, and treat them with respect as the weaker partner and as heirs with you of the gracious gift of life, so that nothing will hinder your prayers.

2 Corinthians 12:8-10 NIV

[8] Three times I pleaded with the Lord to take it away from me [The thorn in his side]. [9] But he said to me, "My grace is sufficient for you, for my power is made perfect in weakness." Therefore I will boast all the more gladly about my weaknesses, so that Christ's power may rest on me. [10] That is why, for

Christ's sake, I delight in weaknesses, in insults, in hardships, in persecutions, in difficulties. For when I am weak, then I am strong.

Elsayed: Any other miraculous example?

Abdullah: Here is yet another dream I had of Jesus when I was a new Christian. My mother-in- law had given me a gift of a diamond encrusted, white gold cross, on a silver chain----but that night I had a dream that showed me the significance of the wooden cross of Jesus Christ.

Chapter 1: Suffering for Christ.

The Wooden Cross

I dreamed that Jesus Christ was going to be preaching at the Vatican and some of my Christian friends and I wanted to get a glimpse of him. In preparation for our trip, we all shaved our heads and put on simple white tunics. Being that I was once a Muslim, I thought to myself, "We all look like a bunch of Muslims ready for the pilgrimage to Mecca."

However, one important detail made us distinctly Christian: we each wore simple wooden crosses around our necks. The crosses were made of rough wood. They were jagged, full of splinters, and they draped over our necks with a white cotton string.

We all stood outside the Vatican, impressed by the size and the architecture of the cathedral. I felt a little embarrassed to be in such an awe-inspiring place with a baldpate, barefoot, and dressed in a simple white tunic.

When the doors of the sanctuary opened, we moved against a crowd of people who were trying to get out. The people were rushing, as if they were exiting a subway train at the Fifty-Ninth Street Station in Manhattan, New York City. A conductor's voice on the loudspeaker said, "Let 'em out first, watch the closing doors!" As we pushed our way inside, I noticed that the people leaving the sanctuary wore ornate gold chains around their necks, and on the chains, hung diamond-studded, golden crucifixes.

Once inside, we again marveled at the architecture—high ceilings and gold everywhere! The people were dressed like soldiers of ancient Rome with gaudy golden helmets, golden armor, and they carried golden spears. I thought that this armor would be useless in real battle, because gold is such a soft metal.

Then I saw a man who looked like Jesus—chubby, smiling, and had red cheeks. I could not tell if it was really Jesus, because he did not resemble the emaciated, suffering, rendition of Christ that I had seen in pictures. Twelve people, who resembled disciples, sat around this man. One turned to our small group and said, "We will show you humble ones what is true joy, so much joy that you will dance on a leaf while it is still on the tree!"

At this remark from the disciple, the man who looked like Jesus smiled at us and nodded in agreement, though he did not say a word. The next moment, the disciples began to sing the hymn, "Oh, Mighty Cross." The Roman soldiers would not sing, but the group from our church immediately joined in. Our voices cracked with emotion; our faces covered with tears of adoration.

As we sang, I clutched the small wooden cross around my neck. Thankful that Jesus had loved me, I took delight when my hand was pierced by a little splinter from my cross. At the same moment my finger was pierced, I could feel the eyes of the man, who resembled Jesus, look at me. He was somehow attuned to every human suffering, even the minor suffering caused by my little wooden splinter. The words he said assured me that he was the living Christ. He said, "I too had a cross, and it too had splinters, but my cross also had nails."

Hearing this, we all knew we were in front of the real Jesus Christ, and we fell at his feet. A wonderful sense of peace covered us. We were all grateful that our crosses were not made of gold, but rather of rough wood. And we were all grateful that our crosses, although they had splinters, they did not have nails.

Elsayed: Wow, I'm speechless! Jesus knew that you had a little splinter in your finger. Is it true that he knows all human suffering? And do we have to suffer a little bit to get to know Jesus better?

Abdullah: Good things come through suffering, especially when we suffer for Christ. Success comes from a delay of gratification, but life's ultimate delay of gratification comes when we transfer our worldly talents and possessions into eternal wealth in the next life. Pastor A.W.Tozer once said, "whatever is given to the Lord Jesus Christ is immediately touched with immortality."

The Contrast between Suffering for Christ, versus Suffering for our Addictions.

What is the need for Christian suffering? Why invite pain and suffering when we instinctively and reflexively avoid pain? There is plenty of suffering in the fallen world in which we live, but we have a choice to either suffer for Jesus, or to suffer for our addictions, temptations, and sin.

I have been treating HIV for more than thirty years, and I have practiced addiction medicine in the South Bronx. In my experience, no one wakes up one morning and declares, "today I want to become a drug addict!" ***Addiction results from a gradual training of our flesh to become intolerant to even a low level of noxious stimuli***. What starts as a natural ***aversion*** to pain, becomes an ***anticipation*** of pain, followed by an anxiety about pain. Anxiety leads to other psychiatric illnesses: depression, paranoia, and sociopathic behavior, just to name a few. We ultimately find ourselves taking extreme measures to make the pain stop, even before it starts, and we want to prevent pain at any cost. These extreme measures feed our addiction, whether it is overeating, gossiping, alcohol, drugs, or whatever.

Next, we have to create a ***web of lies*** so that we can maintain relationships with those who we love, while attempting to still chase our addiction----we learn how to live a double life. How do you know an addict is lying? His lips are moving. Personally, I am an overweight man who hides candy-bars all over the house, so I can eat them when my wife is not looking. She can't understand why my belly is still big and round, despite her feeding me only tofu and rice cakes. Addiction makes us self-centered instead of other- centered; and all of our time, energy, and resources, are used to support our addiction. We develop a mindset that is geared to avoid suffering, and is intolerant to even low levels of pain----or in my case, low levels of hunger. We cringe at just the thought of painful situations----I am terrified by the thought of starvation. Our addictions put us on a mission to feed our flesh; which is the opposite of suffering for Christ, and *feeding our spirit.*

What started as an innocent avoidance of pain, a little appeasement of the flesh, has turned into an all consuming, *'religion' of addiction*. If you do not choose to suffer for Christ, you will unintentionally suffer for your addiction; if you don't stand for God, you will fall for anything that Satan throws at you. My best advice to the self engrossed drug addict is, "stop doing drugs, and use the money that you save to buy a gift for someone that you love." This advice is designed to take the addict's focus away from appeasing his flesh, and diverting it towards building a loving relationship with people, and ultimately a loving relationship with God.

Romans 8:13 NIV [13] For if you live according to the flesh, you will die; but if by the Spirit you put to death the misdeeds of the body, you will live.

We are at war with Satan, and *suffering for Christ is a kind of 'boot camp'* before we go to war. Soldiers do not prepare for war by going to the nail salon for a manicure and a pedicure; instead, they go to boot camp to get stronger and smarter, so that they will be prepared for war. *God takes 'Soldiers in Christ' and strengthens them through bad situations, and suffering.* God uses our pain and suffering to strengthen our faith, and bolster our spirit. If the pain of life does not kill you, it will make your spirit stronger; the alternative, if we succumb to our addictions because we are averse to suffering, we will die a spiritual death, if not also a premature physical death.

There were two thieves who were crucified on crosses that were adjacent to the cross of Jesus. These two thieves represent two kinds of people; although both were suffering, only one chose to suffer for Christ, and the other chose to suffer for his flesh. One of the thieves hurled insults at Jesus; this man had not yet finished *appeasing his flesh*, even though he was being crucified, his arrogance prevented him from receiving the *'good news,'* that is, the *'Gospel.'* The other thief had spiritual introspection, and although he too was getting crucified, this second thief desired to *appease his spirit.* The second thief chose to be crucified with Christ, and Jesus responded by offering him the kingdom of God. Can you guess which of these two thieves was 'born again?'

Elsayed: It's kind a like the saying, "if you don't stand for something, you'll fall for anything!"

Abdullah: God knows the end from the beginning, and so He is not perturbed by our suffering. If we live by faith, abiding in God's promises, miracles happen: inhalation causes exhalation, poverty causes surplus, weakness causes strength, suffering causes deliverance, sickness causes healing, persecution causes adoption into God's family, suffering for Christ releases the joy in our life, crucifying our flesh causes us to love our enemies, and finally, worldly death causes eternal life for the child of God.

Isaiah 54:10 NIV

[10] Though the mountains be shaken and the hills be removed, yet my unfailing love for you will not be shaken nor my covenant of peace be removed," says the Lord, who has compassion on you.

Abdullah: The Bible tells us "to live as Christ, and to die as gain." That means we should live by the example of Christ, and when we die we gain eternity——and that transaction more than offsets the loss of our physical life.

Pick up your Cross and Follow Jesus.

God does not call the qualified, he qualifies the called. It's not about your ability, it's about your availability.

Stop your whining!

Life is supposed to have a little pain and suffering ----

That is how you know you are not in heaven.

Deal with it!

Jesus said, "pick up your cross and follow me."

Elsayed: What does it mean to be crucified with Christ?

Abdullah: Jesus died on the cross for me, so as they say in the Bronx, "I would take a bullet for that man!" Not only would it be honorable to die for Jesus, but when you woke up in the next life you would see angels, and you will join them praising God forever, and ever. That is a far cry from being a suicide bomber, blowing up innocent lives, and seeking 72 ugly virgins in the hereafter. That is also a far cry from the atheist, Who thinks that life after death is nothing more than fake news, and when he dies the worms get the last say, because there is no eternal life. Without God in the picture, the atheist lives his life with little, or no, accountability. Why bother pleasing a god that doesn't exist?

We Christians do not want to grieve God because of our sin, and when we stand before God in the next life, we want to hear God say, "welcome my good and faithful servant." Those words by God are what motivates us not to sin, even though our salvation does not depend on having our good works outweigh our sins; it was Jesus's work on the cross that atoned for our sins.

Elsayed: What did you specifically give up to follow Christ?

Abdullah: You mean besides the persecution from my Muslim relatives, and the certain death I would face if I return to the Middle East to tout Christianity?

Elsayed: Yeah. Besides that stuff!

Abdullah: My wife and I gave up a lucrative private practice in order for us to move to a clinic in the South Bronx. We give our time, money, energy, and talents to fight the works of Satan in the South Bronx.

Elsayed: What is the evidence that your ministry is making a difference in the South Bronx?

Abdullah: Sometimes we get a glimpse of the positive changes in the lives of our friends from the Bronx. Such was the case with Curtis "Sweetpea" Ferguson, original gangster, and one of the cofounders of the Bloods Gang. Curtis was a killer, but he is now my brother in Christ. And since he came to the Lord, the Bronx has become a safer place.

Curtis has a new perspective on life. He says that trouble has a purpose----it is a catalyst to move you into a new phase of your life. Whenever there is trouble in a believer's life, you can be sure that God is getting ready to do something great in us, and through us.

Curtis wrote this saying: "when God wants to do **something good**, He starts with a ***difficulty***; when He wants to do ***something great***, He begins with an ***impossibility***. This is to let everyone know that what is impossible for us is easy for God----He is more than able."

Elsayed: How did you relate with the founder of the Bloods gang?

Abdullah: The first day I met him I called him "a little bitch."

Elsayed: You said what?

Abdullah: Yeah. He was crying like a little bitch when they drew his blood in my clinic. So I told him to "stop crying like a little bitch!" Then he told me who he was and I started crying like a little bitch. Needless to say, where it not for the love of Jesus, I would've been dead long before I was divorced from my wife. But praise God, I'm not dead, and I am not divorced after 35 years of marriage, despite more than a few close calls.

Elsayed: It is only by the grace of God that we can accomplish the big things and the little things in life. Only by the grace of God can a fool like you stay alive in the South Bronx!

Abdullah: I take nothing for granted. Breathing is an example of God's grace in the little things that we take for granted. If we were just to inhale, or if we were just to exhale, we would suffocate. But by the grace of God not only is there a cycle of respiration, but the Lord provides us with red blood cells, and hemoglobin within the red blood cells, so that we can bring oxygen to our brain, heart, muscles, and all the cells of our body, and remove the harmful carbon dioxide. Most of the time we don't even realize that we are breathing, yet if we were to stop breathing we would die within minutes——the seen, and unseen, grace of God is the only reason why we are still living. The Lord, our God, is in charge of all cyclical processes in our life:

Ecclesiastes 3:1 NIV

[1] There is a time for everything, and a season for every activity under the heavens.

Genesis 8:22 NIV

[22] "As long as the earth endures, seedtime and harvest, cold and heat, summer and winter, day and night will never cease."

Elsayed: Muslims pray five times a day, how often do you pray?

Abdullah: Now that I walk with the Lord, my life has become one continuous prayer, and I confidently expect that my loving God will keep us safe, and married, and He will keep His promises to us, as it is written in the Bible. In the end, when my wife and I have fulfilled our unified purpose on earth, God will call us home, and we will gladly go to Him, just to hear Him say, "well done, my good and faithful servant."

Chapter2: Suffering through Marriage.

Elsayed: Your wife has worked with you all these years in the South Bronx. she definitely had your back. What makes a good wife? How do I know if I found the right person?

Abdullah: In answer to your question, you don't "find" the right person, just like you don't find God——God finds you after you ready your heart with peace, love, and faith. Instead of finding the right person, you become the right person, and as a couple you become the right people. The Bible says, after marriage a man and a woman become "one flesh." What started as two individuals becomes one couple.

Marriage is medicine for loneliness. The right Medicine, at the right dose, can cure your blues; but too much of even the right medicine can be poisonous; and even a small amount of the wrong medicine will kill you fast.

Having common goals in life is actually more important than being in love. This is because no one really knows what love is when we are young and foolish, but it is easier to quantify the goals that will keep us moving in the right direction as husband and wife. The greatest goal, of course, is to seek first the kingdom of God as a couple. The Bible says if you seek God first then he will grant you all that you need in your life.

And finally, there is the 'risk versus benefit' analysis. My girlfriend, who later became my wife, asked, "are we ever going to get married one day?" To which I answered, "if the reasons for us to stay together outweigh the reasons for us to move apart, then we will definitely stay together and be married."

Overtime, it hurt too much to leave her, and it felt just right to stay. Love was beginning to gel in our lives.There were more reasons to stay, more common goals, and the best goal was to serve God together for life. And so we got married in three months after I met her. My friends and my family said we were crazy. My oldest son, Adam, helped us make the decision to get married long before he was even born. It seems that Adam was conceived in a little town, just outside of wedlock! Neither of us believed in abortion. So, as much of a pain in the ass my son Adam has turned out to be, he was and still is, the glue that holds our family together!

The turning point for me was when I found out just how much my girlfriend loved God. Whenever she talked about God she would have tears in her eyes from a strong spiritual desire to love Him. I fell in love with a woman who loved God more than she loved her own life, and more than she loved me. I knew the ride would be bumpy because we were not of the same religion, but the most important thing was our shared goal to seek God, and to love God.

I convinced her to Convert to Islam, which she did for the first 10 years of our marriage, followed by converting back to born-again Christianity at year 10, followed by my conversion to born- again Christianity, by year 14 of our marriage. It was a rocky ride between year 10 and year 14, to say the least!

Thirty-five years later, the rocks on the road of our marriage have become smaller, and smaller, and now they are just pebbles by the grace of God. After all these years I have the authority to tell her to "cut it out," whenever she stresses the small stuff (the pebbles). Sometimes I take the batteries out of my hearing aids.

God honors our little house because we honor his grand kingdom. Joseph said, in the Bible, "as for me and my house, we will serve the Lord."

Elsayed: and what about your wife? How has she kept you on the straight and narrow path?

Abdullah: The Bible says, "Iron sharpens iron," but sometimes the hammer of marriage is used to forge iron.

Abdullah: In God's economy there are no wasted events----everything happens for a reason in your life, even the problems. To refine metal you have to put it in the fire; to forge iron you have to hit it with a hammer. *Marriage is such a hammer*. The Bible says, "iron sharpens iron," and to be sure, many of my spiritual epiphanies occurred at Christian men's retreats, but my wife accomplishes significant changes in my life when she wields the *marital hammer*.

Raising a family will raise the temperature for the melting process, rendering the iron more malleable, easily forged by the marital hammer. Recently, she chased away all of those scoundrels, who I called my friends, until the only friend I had left was Jesus. How could I write if I was always wasting time, hanging out with my buddies?

My wife once complained to God, while contemplating divorce ten years into our marriage, "Lord, I asked you for a Christian husband, and look what you gave me!"

The Lord answered her, and corrected her, saying, " You asked me to give you a *'good'* husband, you never specifically asked for a *'Christian'* man."

After 14 years of marriage I became a Christian. She just had to wait four more years for the Lord to answer to her prayers.

Elsayed: For a while there she really didn't want you as a husband. She was complaining to God!

Abdullah: Yeah, pretty girls have lots of options—— they are like the fentanyl dealers in the South Bronx: those dealers are sought after even if their product kills. The dealers buy T-shirts for their customers that read, "If found dead you should go to my drug dealer, call him at:

555-FENTANYL. He's got the good shit!"

Abdullah: She didn't even want the guy before me. Did I ever tell you that she was engaged to marry some other guy, from the Philippines, when I first met her?

But I asked her, "can I be your little dog until your big dog comes?"

Fast forward 35 years, and the other guy is ancient history! Who's your Big-Dog now? Woof! Woof! Who's your daddy?

Her arms are too short to box with God, but nonetheless, she had the divorce lawyer's phone number on speed-dial. Here is an essay which explains our complicated relationship:

The Vine, the Gardener, and the Pruning Shears (my wife's elbows).

The Bible is full of stories of bumbling prophets who nevertheless were used to advance God's perfect will: Abraham sinned with the slave girl, Hagar, and yet he became the father of all nations; David sinned with Bathsheba, and yet he produced a lineage that led to Jesus. There is no wastage in God's economy, all that is expected of us is that we abide in God, and in return, God will abide in us, and He will order our steps.

John 15:5
Jesus said, "I am the vine and you are the branches; whoever abides in me and I in him, he it is that bears much fruit, for apart from me you can do nothing."

Jesus is the trunk of the vine, we are the branches growing in every direction from the trunk, and God is the gardener who prunes the branches. God prunes away branches that have withered, or are lacking fruit, or are growing too aggressively, or are growing in the wrong direction. The pruning is done to maintain the productivity and the health of the vine. Put in another way, God chastens the one he loves and seeks to make us perfect. God will not protect us from trouble if that trouble will ultimately lead us to perfection. As long as we abide in the vine, God can redeem us no matter what mistakes we make along the way.

I submit that the pruning shears used by God in my life are the two elbows of my wife. For the past thirty years, whenever God saw it fit to prune my branches, He picked up my wife's skinny, sharp elbows. These elbows find their way to my ribs whenever I'm on the verge of making a costly mistake, such as:

1) falling asleep in church.

2) talking too much about myself at a party.

3) grabbing the largest piece of meat at the party.

4) falling asleep on the couch after I've eaten the largest piece of meat at the party.

5) drinking too much.

6) driving too fast.

7) drinking much, and driving fast.

8) glancing at a pretty girl while walking in the mall.

9) five minutes later, this time wearing dark sunglasses, glancing at a pretty girl while walking in the mall.

10) doing anything that might jeopardize my life, or my relationship with God, or my relationship with my wife. That covers a lot of evil!

God made Eve from Adam's rib, that's why I sometimes like to call my wife "ribby," or, "ribeye (after my favorite large piece of meat)," or, "yo ribby!" Somehow, she never acknowledges me, unless.... Oh no, here comes another elbow!

Men and women are equals. God made Eve from Adam side, not from above his head, or from below is feet – – – we are equal but we are definitely not the same. Viva la difference! Hey, wait a minute! I just figured out what my wife is doing when she elbows me in the ribs – – – she's trying to crack through my exterior, and climb back into my chest cavity, so that she can once again become one with my ribs! Isn't that romantic?

Elsayed: What if my wife doesn't want to crawl into my chest cavity? Can I have buyers remorse? Can I get a divorce? So, if my future wife, God forbid, can't have any children for some reason, and procreation is the main reason for sex, is that grounds for divorce?

Abdullah: No, you can't divorce your wife just because she can't get pregnant. Jesus said that adultery is the only reason for divorce, because the marriage commitment/covenant was desecrated. There is no easy way out of marriage once you have entered the marriage covenant. Husbands and wives must show grace, mercy and forgiveness toward one another. God is not in favor of division, but rather He wants unity despite hard circumstances.

The Bible is full of stories of barren women being able to give birth after the couple started to pray for the miracle of pregnancy. Abraham and Sarah were 100 years old when they had their first child, and Abraham is known as "the father of all nations."

Procreation isn't the main reason for sex. Sex is also a celebration of being one flesh with your spouse. You are celebrating an intimate relationship with one other person, in a manner that mirrors our unique relationship with God.

Sex is an act of worship, and children are a blessing from God, but there needs to be a commitment to stay together and raise a family.

Timing a family is difficult. The best time for a woman to give birth, from a physiological perspective, is between the ages of 20 and 30; on the other hand, men can procreate as long as they have a sufficient sperm count, and these soldiers know how to swim straight.

Not everyone wants to have a family, nor should everyone have a family. An elderly man shouldn't have children if he cannot spend time raising them because he is too weak and feeble. If a 30 year old woman gives birth to a female child, that puts her future menopause in alignment with her daughter's future premenstrual syndrome——there will be lots of fights and big trouble in twenty years.

The best time to have a marriage and start a family is when you're too young and stupid to realize what you're getting into. That's probably in your mid 20s, for a woman, and in your mid 30s for a man. Men stay stupid longer. Once you start having a family you need to pray a lot for God's help, because life just got a whole lot more complicated. That's why it is important to finish school, get a job, and be a 'go getter' before having children, because children rightly will occupy much of your time and effort.

Above all, don't be a polygamist, because this grieves God. Your Muslim father was a polygamist, but every married man who views pornography is also a polygamist. The lewd images on a computer screen take away time, energy, and trust from his wife and family. it's hard enough for a married couple to stay together, the forces of evil are all around, but sex between a husband and a wife is God's glue to help keep us together. That glue cannot be shared with anyone outside of the marriage, and definitely not wasted on Internet pornography. "Oh, but my wife's mean to me when she's having her period, so I go on the Internet and look at porn."

Don't do porn! If your wife is cruel to you, do this instead: suck it up, and keep it moving! Find a way to make your wife smile again. Spend your time, energy, and prayers in an effort to build up your family life. Real men don't require Vaseline. They require duct tape, gorilla glue, and 10W40. Real men fix things, they glue the broken pieces, and they take away rust from the past, and keep it moving.

The broken pieces may be from her childhood trauma, you must gather the pieces and apply duct tape and gorilla glue. Her innocent childhood emotions may have gathered rust from years of anxiety, depression, and mistrust——nothing that a little 10W40 can't fix. A little anointing oil can return her to smooth innocence. A good man knows how to troubleshoot his family, his wife, and himself, and he keeps it moving. Moving toward the kingdom of God.

Elsayed: Hey Doc, you're just another red blooded American guy! How do you get by? Do you just "yes" her to death and then do whatever you want, like most guys?

Abdullah: No, heaven's no! I strive to become more, and more, connected to Jesus so that there are fewer, and fewer, things that she can find objectionable about me. I let her shake the sin out of my life instead of allowing it to be stirred into the mixture that we call marriage—— that is how James Bond liked his martinis, "shaken not stirred."

Shaken, Not Stirred.

In the old spy thriller James Bond movies, Bond famously liked his martini "shaken not stirred!" For the top British spy, code name 007, who had a license to kill, it was not an option to stir the ingredients of his martini together. He wanted all the solid ingredients to be pushed to the bottom where they could be discarded before he drank from the emulsified top ingredients of his martini that had been vigorously shaken together. Hence, his martini had to be shaken, not stirred. Bond's drink had to be homogenized, although his love life was far from being monogamous. James Bond had lipstick on his collar, not snots from his two-year-old's nose.

Yet we look up to him because he fought the good fight, and ran the good race, for his Queen and his country, Great Britain.

The character of James Bond never planned to live much beyond the age of forty, nor did he ever plan to have a wife and kids, or a house with a white picket fence. If he ever married, Bond would have made the marriage counselor rich, but there was something very right in the way he drank his martinis——shaken not stirred. The ingredients of his life were brought together for a unified goal, and that was to serve the British queen at all costs. James Bond had only one goal, and all other purposes were to be left in the mixing decanter, shaken out of his life, not anymore in the martini glass from which he was to drink.

We can get behind a guy who lives for a uniformly right purpose, that is, if he is serving the right authority. Think of Jesus Christ, whose only purpose was to be offered up as a sacrifice for all human sin, and God was his authority. Jesus famously said to God, "let this cup [of crucifixion] be taken away from me, but Lord, let your will be done, not mine." Now, it may be sacrilegious, comparing James Bond to Jesus Christ, but both had a one-track mind, and both were determined to carry out their assignment.

The Biblical book of Hebrews could be summed up in a single phrase: "fight the good fight, and run the good race." The book of Hebrews also talks about being 'shaken and not stirred:' saying, do not 'stir' your addictions in the same drink that you call godliness——be of one, unified, Godly purpose, and 'shake' all non-essential people, places, and things out of your life. That sounds like advice from an alcoholics anonymous meeting, where they advise, "avoid people, places, and things that will lead you back to your addiction." Don't fight to keep an addiction, instead you must fight to keep a unified goal for serving in the kingdom of God.

Don't try to serve two masters, God and your addiction; but seek first the kingdom of God and his righteousness and all good things God will grant you. If you put God first then you will have fought the good fight and you will have won the race—— the race we call life.

Hebrews 12:26-28 NIV

[26] At that time his [God's] voice shook the earth, but now he has promised, "Once more I will shake not only the earth but also the heavens." [27] The words "once more" indicate the removing of what can be shaken---that is, created things---so that what cannot be shaken may remain. [28] Therefore, since we are receiving a kingdom that cannot be shaken, let us be thankful, and so worship God acceptably with reverence and awe.

But how does God equip us to fight the good fight and run the good race? God trains us as if we were Olympic athletes. Discipline for an athlete results in better performance during the race.

Hebrews 12:11-15. NIV

[11] No discipline seems pleasant at the time, but painful. Later on, however, it produces a harvest of righteousness and peace for those who have been trained by it. [12] Therefore, strengthen your feeble arms and weak knees. [13] "Make level paths for your feet," so that the lame may not be disabled, but rather healed. [14] Make every effort to live in peace with everyone and to be holy; without holiness no one will see the Lord. [15] See to it that no one falls short of the grace of God and that no bitter root grows up to cause trouble and defile many.

How else does God prepare us for life? God chastens the one he loves. He uses people, places, and things to make tough adjustments in our lives. God uses wives, husbands, and even children to give us life lessons. Those who take advice will learn and thrive, but those who reject advice from loved ones will have Satan as a guide. Broken marriages, child and spousal abuse, this is what happens to a person who does not take loving advice, and instead clings to his addictions. No one should marry the drug dealer, but it is good to remain married to the wife of your youth. Even if your wife nags, at least she doesn't kill you with fentanyl.

Hebrews 12:5-8. NIV

It says, "My son, do not make light of the Lord's discipline, and do not lose heart when he rebukes you, [6] because the Lord disciplines the one he loves, and he chastens everyone he accepts as his son." [7] Endure hardship as discipline; God is treating you as his children. For what children are not disciplined by their father? [8] If you are not disciplined---and everyone undergoes discipline---then you are not legitimate, not true sons and daughters at all.

James bond, being an international man of mystery, had a lot of girlfriends but no wife. He was never sure if he would be dead in the next hour, or day, so he kept jumping from one femme fatale to the next. Frequently, his girlfriends, who pretended to love him, were really out to kill him, but they never succeeded, or the fantasy of James Bond would have ended far too abruptly. My wife, on the other hand, is not trying to kill me, even though sometimes I may feel that she is. Quite the reverse, my wife is a ray of God's light shining on my path. God sent her to order my steps and for me to learn love, patience, and humility. While I'm married to her, I can't afford to be a bad ass like James Bond.

Hebrews 12:16-18. NIV

[16] See that no one is sexually immoral, or is godless like Esau, who for a single meal sold his inheritance rights as the oldest son. [17] Afterward, as you know, when he wanted to inherit this blessing, he was rejected. Even though he sought the blessing with tears, he could not change what he had done.

James bond was not looking for a soulmate, with whom he would spend a long happy life. His motto was, "slam bam, thank you ma'am." His motto was never, "happy wife, happy life," or, "it's more important to be happy than to be right," or, "if mama ain't happy, nobody's happy!" James bond solved all his problems by shooting people that he didn't agree with. There was never a 'mama Bond,'or a 'baby Bond' in the movies that depicted a suave British spy who had only one purpose, and that was to serve the Queen of Great Britain.

Hey, but what about the rest of us guys! What about the real male heroes, who safely reach the age of fifty, and are balding and fat, but are happily married and are faithful to the wife of their youth? Real heroes drink beer not martinis, they scratch their beer bellies while watching football on Sundays, and instead of pulling triggers, they will ask you to pull their finger after they eat peanuts.

I am sixty years old, bald and fat, but I am a real hero to my wife, three kids, and six grandkids. I am a real hero even if my wife and kids won't easily admit it. I am once married, for thirty-five years, to the wife of my youth. I was twenty-five years old when I got married to my soulmate. I was so young, my ego was so fragile. She converted from Christianity to Islam for convenience and for harmonious love, so she could marry me, a Muslim. When I first laid my eyes on her, I said, "Allah has favored me!," but after thirty-five years of marriage, and a new religion, I look at the same woman and say, "the Lord is trying to shake up my life and whip me into shape!"

I was 137 pounds when I married my wife, years later I ballooned up to 237 pounds. At first, my wife would say, "you're so skinny I could break you like a stick," and then she would say, "you're so fat I could roll you down a hill!" I asked her, "I must've been just the right weight for you, somewhere in between 137 and 237 pounds, why didn't you pay me a compliment?" She quickly responded, "I didn't need to tell you anything when you were perfect. Your head might've swollen up! When you used to play basketball you had a round ass and a flat belly, now your ass has rotated to the front."

James bond never had to put up with disparaging nicknames from his women, such as the ones my wife gave me: she called me "turkey neck," and, "hillbilly teeth," and because my bald spot has a strange, resilient line of hair right down the middle, she calls me, "butt-head." But I don't mind. At least we got the marriage counselor to gag on her laughter, while she tried to remain professional during a counseling session where my wife called me "turkey neck," quickly followed by the gobble-gobble sound that a turkey makes. But I don't mind the disparaging nicknames, because unlike James Bond's girlfriends who were trying to kill him, my wife was trying to shake me up and make me better. You see, while James Bond was busy shaking martinis to make his drink better, my wife was shaking her husband to make him better.

But things were not always peachy in our marriage. If I were a peach tree, my wife would systematically shake my tree until the fruits of Islam all fell down. Sometimes she would shake my tree so much that not only the fruit fell, but also some of the leaves. But that's okay, in time the leaves would grow back stronger, and the pruning she did made my branches grow straight towards the light of God. I have thirty-five lumps on my head, one for every year of marriage, like tree-rings. I just take my lumps and keep it moving. Heroes take their lumps. On good days frying pans make eggs and bacon, on bad days frying pans make lumps on a husband's head. Like tree rings they occur once for every year of marriage.

Ten years into our marriage she converted back to Christianity, and fourteen years into our marriage she told me that it was important to raise our children as Christians and not Muslims. Needless to say, this almost caused a divorce. My wife had the divorce lawyer's phone number on speed dial. I was like a martini in her hand, which was 'shaken but not stirred.' She refused to stir components of Islam into the mixture, refusing to let my past Islamic fruit spoil her drink. You can't mix ocean water with fresh water and expect to call the mixture 'Poland Spring.'

Did I mention that my wife prayed me into the kingdom of God? For three weeks at 3 AM every morning she would wake up and plead the blood of Jesus over me. She would also anoint my forehead with oil as I slept. At the end of the third week I had a dream in which I saw Jesus.

You don't see Jesus and stay the same. The next day I was saved.

But my wife wasn't finished shaking me. As a Christian in good standing I joined a men's group. My wife made it her responsibility to call five or six men from this group, explaining what each should say to me, speaking her words into my life, through them. The men couldn't throw my wife out of the men's group, so they threw me out instead. True story.

My wife has never stopped training me to be the Olympic athlete that she believes I can be. She did the math——when I thrive, then she thrives, because she's my wife in good standing. I wouldn't take advice from a femme fatale who was trying to kill me, like all of James Bond's evil girlfriends. My wife is my queen and, "long live the queen!"

Elsayed: "treat others as they would want to be treated----not necessarily the way you want to be treated." I never heard this saying before. I absolutely love it.

Abdullah: That's called 'the platinum rule of marriage,' as opposed to Jesus's 'golden rule,' which is to "do unto others as you would have them do unto you." Why the upgrade? It is because we are to treat our wives better than we would treat anyone else in the world. The pedestal we make for our wives is very high because she is important, and it is very heavy, so she can't pick it up and throw it at you when she's mad.

Elsayed: What is the secret to staying married thirty-five years?

Abdullah: Here is a love letter I wrote to my wife.

Thirty-five years and counting! Letter to my wife and soulmate.

Proverb: "the wise man foresees trouble and hides himself. " note: the wise man doesn't go looking for trouble, if trouble finds him he doesn't try to fight it; but rather, he humbly hides himself from trouble. Marriage is a way that we hide each other inside the will of God, through God's covenant; yet marriage is a hotbed of conflict. It is easy to get married but it is hard to stay married.

Avoidance of unnecessary conflict is wise, but marriage is a necessary conflict. Without marriage you could not obtain the goals that God has ordained for every man and woman. Loving reconciliation of our conflicts is worth a few black eyes to our ego and pride. Marriage is an institution created by God. God intends for us to leave our biological family and become 'one flesh' with our spouse so that he can accomplish his will in our lives.

Some, like the apostle Paul, may say that it is wise to steer clear of all trouble, remain celibate, but it is better to prepare oneself to become marriageable, even if you never intend to marry. We make this preparation through self searching, patience, hard work, and perseverance. When marriage finally happens between two unselfish people, who are on the same page to serve the Lord, Satan cannot put a wedge between them and they can accomplish great things for the kingdom of God.

I could give a long list of people who had bad intentions for us, but through God's hedge of protection, and our clinging to God's will, and to each other, we were able to persevere. There is no other woman that I'd like to go to battle with other than you. You are the love of my life, my soulmate, and God's mercy and providence in my life.

The next 35 years will be better than the last 35 years! I plan to stay by your side, to see what God's plan is for us and how the future unfolds like a beautiful, fragrant flower.

Chapter 3: Love is the Glue.

Elsayed: very touching – – – Not! What about your kids? Tell me something about the spiritual relationship that you have with your kids.

Abdullah: Sometimes, husbands and wives can become thorns in one another's side, but if they can stick together the couple can provide a strong platform for God to do great things to advance His kingdom. This can be said about marriage, even if at the moment it doesn't feel successful: "when husband and wife are on the same page, and Satan cannot put a wedge between them, they can accomplish great and mighty things for the kingdom of God." One of the most important accomplishments is to raising God fearing children.

At a Christian men's retreat the pastor gave this warning to all of the patriarchs and family men in the room, he said, "one day you will stand before God, and He will ask you for an account of your wife's sins, and your kid's sins, as well as your own sins. God will hold you accountable for anyone who carries your family name." I never thought to question if that advise was strictly Biblical, but nevertheless, the scripture says, "as for me and my house, we will serve the Lord."

The best way you can love your kids is to first love your God, and then love your wife, and then love your kids. They will learn by example. Here is a story about my carpentry hobby, which my son, Raza, imitated. I started to like carpentry even before I knew that Jesus was a carpenter.

Jesus too was a carpenter

Twenty years ago my father showed me a shaker style bench which I had built for him. Dad asked me if I knew how the surface of the bench got damaged with little punctate marks.

I remembered that the marks had been made by my son, Raza. He was only four years old when he tried to imitate me by using a meat tenderizer like a hammer. "It doesn't matter," I said to my father, " a bench is just a bench and Raza is my son."

20 years later my son Raza is building his own carpentry project. He is building a cold frame for planting seedlings.

As I came closer I realized something peculiar about the workbench that he was using to support his project. The workbench was not a workbench at all, but rather it was composed of two of my shaker benches that I built 20 years ago. The same ones he had hammered with the meat tenderizer when he was only four years old.

Raza was once again hammering on top of my bench, only this time he was also sawing, and sanding, and painting. As Raza's project was coming together, my benches were gradually getting destroyed.

I didn't know if I should get angry at my son, but suddenly a little voice came into my head. The voice said, "Your son is building upon that which you built. Even as you diminish he shall increase."

Jesus too was a carpenter, and he also was the cornerstone upon which the church was built. Through the sacrifice of Jesus Christ the world has seen great gain.

The small, still voice was calling me to be an unselfish father despite the burden of fatherhood. A good father, and also a good mother, will die a little every day for their children.

Raza glanced up from his work, perhaps looking to see if I was angry at him.

I just looked at him reassuredly, saying, "It doesn't matter," I said to my son, "a bench is just a bench and Raza, you are my son."

Elsayed: It sounds like love is the glue that holds your family together, but you also have to earn a living. How can you seek God and support a family at the same time?

Elsayed: How do you stay motivated? What sort of goals should I be setting for myself? Strictly monetary based for now while establishing my career? I know you said when you have faith God provides for you but it seems like you were ambitious even before your strong connection with Him.

Abdullah: Are you are aware that most of us don't fully utilize the Holy Spirit power that lives in our hearts; are you aware that we only use about 2% of our brains? How do we maximize the power of our hearts and our brains? I could do an infomercial for having a relationship with Jesus, but Satan wouldn't let it sell.

The Bible has the answer. Simply put, worship God and think of beautiful things.

Some people think that spirituality is a big waste of time, but the greatest epiphanies in my life have come while I was seeking God with all of my heart, mind, and strength. If I didn't worship God and think of beautiful things, instead, I would worship my own foolish ambitions and dwell on negative thoughts. In short, I would become a slave of Satan.

What is the rat race? It is a bunch of negative people, who worship their own progress, while never thinking to advance the kingdom of God. The opposite of this is when we follow the scripture that says, "seek first the kingdom of God, and His righteousness, and all of these things will be added onto you."

You can chew gum and walk at the same time. You can seek God, worship him, and think of beautiful things, even while you pursue your education, advancement at your job, and a family life. The spiritual and secular worlds are not mutually exclusive. God wants you to prosper in this life, and also in the life here after. Worldly success is linked to our spiritual success. I will give you a personal example.

Remember, I told you that God sometimes comes to us in dreams and visions. I often wakeup at three or four o'clock in the morning with an answer to one of my burning questions. For instance, during the early days of the HIV epidemic, I once woke up with a dream of a spider's web. I instantly knew, in my heart and in my brain, that God was telling me to combine Ritonivir with other protease inhibitors to get a boosting effect that would help me treat my HIV patients, and to prevent them from dying. When I attended an HIV conference that was held by the makers of Ritonivir, Abbott laboratories, I looked like a genius. I was everyone's hero when I stated that I combined this medication with other protease inhibitors and achieved startling good results in over 100 patients.

God's wisdom, not my own, was revealed to me through a dream. It might've taken me 30 years to get to that point without God's help. I have an unfair advantage over other researchers in the field of HIV. And my clinic has a success rate of over 90%, which is unheard of in the South Bronx. To God be the glory if my patients do well, to me be the reason if they do poorly. I'm just a man, I make mistakes, but God is the master physician.

Finally, worshiping God and focusing on all that is beautiful in life, makes life much more fun. I love to marvel at the trees, the streams, the animals, the insects, and all that God has created. God has a sense of humor, and it is fine if we share this humor as we ponder the perplexities of life. Jesus must've known every stupid idea that was going through his disciples heads, as they were thinking, but the joke's on us. God wants us to live a fully joyful, productive life on earth, followed by a total worship party, forever and ever, in heaven. What could be better than that?

Abdullah: The Bible simply says, "God is love." There is a special place in your heart for God's love.

Heart Space for Love.

Did you ever try to fit a square peg into a round hole? You do that every time you sin.

Your heart was made for heaven and not earth.

That is why you cannot please your Spirit while you please your Flesh.

The addictions and the trophies of this world can never fill the space in your heart that God made specifically for His love.

You can never fully appreciate God's love until you are in heaven, but even a little glimpse of God's love on earth can make everything right for us, without it nothing is right.

If you are blind to God's love, on this side of eternity, then you will always underestimate God's plan for you, and you will always live way below the privilege that God offers only to his children.

And you will have missed God's calling on your life.

Without God's love you will always be misunderstood by others, and you will even misunderstand yourself. There will be corruption and confusion.

If you are without love people will judge you harshly, because they can see right through you, down to your evil intentions for them. They see your selfishness, disrespect, ingratitude, and arrogance.

Without God's love you may even start to hate yourself.

Without love you might even start to think that life isn't worth living.

You may entertain thoughts of suicide.

But let not your heart be troubled. God is here to comfort you through His Holy Spirit. Only love can conquer hate. God's love chases away every evil, and turns destruction into blessings.

God's love is the golden rule——

He made you to love Him,

He made you to love yourself,

He made you to love your neighbor as yourself. Love is the very reason why God made you.

Elsayed: Ok, Love of God is important, love of family is important, what about faith?

Abdullah: I was baptized in the Hudson River, by Pastor Carl, at a Christian men's retreat. It was a cold and breezy day, in late November, but strangely I felt warm. My recollection was that I was sheltered from the wind by a semicircle of my brothers in Christ, who were on the shore with outstretched arms, praying for me, and singing the old Christian hymn, 'I have decided to follow Jesus....no turning back....no turning back." My faith in God for the future is strong.

Slowly, over many years, I won over my Muslim relatives. It seems they wanted to share in the kind of peace that I had. They wanted to be a part of God's family. And although no one has outwardly converted from Islam to Christianity, my relatives appreciate the change that they saw in me since I converted. They are more interested in my example than my lectures, or in the spiritual books that I have written. They see my strong my faith.

After my Muslim family stopped persecuting me, I started getting second guessed buy my own kids. My oldest son, Adam, went to a liberal university and promptly became an atheist, now I think he has upgraded to being a Hindu. My daughter, Tahira, married a pastor, so she is all right. My other son, Raza, is also a Christian, and has given us the least trouble, but all of my kids were once teenagers. All teenagers think that they know better than their parents, and they make their parents suffer through the 'hormonal' teenage years. Faith is a muscle that grows through the struggles in life. No pain, no gain.

These are seven pieces of advise for growing faith in your family:

1) *Lead* by example, and with humility.
2) *Love* them unconditionally.
3) *Pray* for them incessantly.
4) *Advise* them only when they ask for it.
5) *Be patient with* the annoying things that they do wrong.

6) ***Give thanks*** for the little things that they do right.

7) Let the Holy Spirit do the work in their lives; do not try to become the Holy Spirit in someone's life.

A very wise deacon at our church, an Indian fellow, named Mammen, gave this explanation for why we had such a hard family life, he said, "one of you is a first generation Christian from a long ancestry of Muslims, and the other is a first generation Christian from a long ancestry of Catholics. The first generation Christians always have the hardest time; however, God knew what he was doing when He brought you both together. Life is hard, but don't lose sight of the great plan that God has in store for you and your family. Keep the faith."

Through it all, my life has gone well whenever I kept my eyes on the Lord, with strong faith. I would find peace and joy whenever I sought to obey God and serve man. Whenever I sought to advance God's great Kingdom, God would keep His promise and advance my own little kingdom. God encourages me through His word, And as it is written in the book of Esther, "you were born for a time just like this." When I feel crushed by the burden of life, I meditate on these four scriptures:

Matthew 11:28-30 NIV

[28] "Come to me, all you who are weary and burdened, and I will give you rest. [29] Take my yoke upon you and learn from me, for I am gentle and humble in heart, and you will find rest for your souls. [30] For my yoke is easy and my burden is light."

Philippians 4:19 NIV

[19] And my God will meet all your needs according to the riches of his glory in Christ Jesus.

Matthew 6:26 NIV

[26] Look at the birds of the air; they do not sow or reap or store away in barns, and yet your heavenly Father feeds them. Are you not much more valuable than they?

Colossians 3:12-14 NIV

[12] 12 Therefore, as God's chosen people, holy and dearly loved, clothe yourselves with compassion, kindness, humility, gentleness and patience. [13] Bear with each other and forgive one another if any of you has a grievance against someone. Forgive as the Lord forgave you. [14] 14 And over all these virtues put on love, which binds them all together in perfect unity.

Elsayed: How do you achieve a balance in life?

Abdullah: Read on. I wrote this essay called "love, power, and soundness of mind."

Love, Power, and Soundness of Mind.

Any definition of success must include the Biblical promise of love, power, and soundness of mind. Even from a completely secular perspective, having a successful life requires having all three of these Biblical promises.

2 Timothy 1:7 NIV

[7] For the Spirit God gave us does not make us timid, but gives us power, love and soundness of mind.

Two out of three of these promises will not result in a successful life. Take for example, Howard Hughes. He had power in the form of great wealth, and for a brief period he had love; but then he lost his mind and soon thereafter he lost his wife, his friends, and eventually even his wealth became inconsequential to him, as he became more and more insane. Pursuit of love and power without a sound mind does not lead to successful living.

Having a sound mind and power, but without love is not enough for success: consider an intellectual. His power is his impeccable logic. Sadly, he can not understand why he gets no attention from women on the internet dating site, this despite posting a long list of his accomplishments. He foolishly wonders, "why can't I convince someone to love me?"

Having a sound mind and love, but without power is not enough for success: take for example the ascetic monk who has great love for God, and a sound mind, but he spends all of his days in a monastery and never evangelizes to the lost. He lacks power. Faith without action is dead. He provides no benefit to God's kingdom.

How can we achieve a balance between love, power, and soundness of mind? What are the components of a successful life? How do successful people carry themselves? Do they display power accompanied by a quiet confidence, or do they exhibit peace that is established in love? Even so, too much of a good thing is harmful. Too much power leads to corruption, and absolute power corrupts absolutely. Too much peace starves our ambition, we forget our original goals, we lose our original love, even the love that first brought us peace. The key is knowing what kind of love brings us peace, and what kind of power gives us confidence. Only the love of God brings 'peace beyond understanding,' and the power of God gives confidence that 'I can do all things in Christ who strengthens me.'

The greatest success, the greatest confidence, the greatest peace, comes to those who 'seek first the kingdom of God and all of these things will be added unto you.' Real peace is knowing that circumstances cannot sway or move us because our center of gravity is based on our unity with God. 'Like a tree that is standing by the water, we shall not be moved.' Be like that tree with spiritual roots running deep, securing life-giving water from the river of God's mercy. Be like that tree that is standing by the water, deeply rooted in the river of God's protection, able to survive every drought and every hurricane because of the invisible roots that are deeply intertwined with God's will.

God given peace and confidence are really the same thing because they come from the same source: unity with God. Unfortunately, we cannot have unity with God if we are under the burden of sin. Real confidence is knowing that Jesus has taken away the burden of our sin, sin that was keeping us from being unified with God, sin that was holding us back from reaching our full potential. Only God's plan is perfect. He wants success for us in this world, and our salvation in the life eternal. Good things happen to those who live out God's plan on earth, and what could be the worst thing? We die, and then see Jesus. 'To live as Christ, to die is gain.' We can not lose.

My worldly success has made me a doctor who treats HIV patients in the South Bronx, NYC. But my worldly success also has eternal ramifications. To some of my patients, Christ is the cornerstone of life, to others Christ is a stumbling block. Nevertheless, I have become a little bit of a street preacher, knowing full well that the worst thing that can happen to me is that I become the victim of a drive-by shooting, and then I quickly get to see Jesus. In the meantime, God has granted me the gift of love, power, and soundness of mind.

This is a prayer that I say to my patients: "if you get better it's because of God, if you get worse it's because of me. I'm just an imperfect man trying to heal you, God is the Master physician!

God does not make mistakes and he does not make junk – – – that's why you should never think poorly of yourself. God made you, and he has kept you alive for a time just as this. God has a plan for you, a plan to prosper you today, tomorrow, and forever – – – your job is to find out that plan, to live it, and to learn to live the privileged life that God intends for you. Don't settle for any less! Don't live your life at a level lower than the high privilege that God intends for you. You are the child of the King! If you believe in Jesus then today is your birthday, and you can ask your 'Agape Pape' for anything! Ask him to be unified with his perfect plan for your life. Ask him and you will receive love, power, and soundness of mind. Give Him the glory, and the joy and healing will come to us! "

We have to break the habit of thinking that we can control our lives. We must acknowledge that we do not know all of the variables that control our destiny. Only God knows every variable, yet God's foreknowledge is not causative; just because God knows the decision you're going to make, it doesn't mean you are forced to make that decision. There is always your free will to choose. God's ways are higher than our ways. Love is God's logic, and His love transcends all human wisdom. God does not even use His mind when He solves every human problem, large and small. Love is God's logic. God transforms our reality with a single beat of His loving heart.

God not only gives us the right to come to Him, but He also longs for us to come to Him. Resting on God's promises through prayer helps us to know God's will in our lives, giving us direction, peace, and confidence. His promises are described in His word, so we must study the Bible and pray with expectancy----holding God to His promises.

Prayer and fasting give us a direct access to God. Although our hard work is admirable, when we work we accomplish a little, when we pray God accomplishes a lot. God has 'a plan to prosper us,' for we are the children of a King and it is our birthday! We can ask Him for anything, for great power, great love, great soundness of mind, and He promises to grant it, as long as we strive to advance His kingdom, and give Him all of the glory.

The Biblical promise of love, power, and soundness of mind, is a promise to who? It is a promise to you. You who first realized today that you are a child of the King, and it is your birthday!

Chapter 4: Faith.

Faith Like A Child.

Human beings innately think that they have a 'right to be right.' We have **free will**. We want to be the controllers of our own destiny. We want to be in the driver seat while we are careening down the highway of life. We think that we are in total control, but there's ice on the road and our tires are bald. God has a driving school, and God's school has only one rule, **"don't drive faster than your angels can fly."** Don't drive so fast, that when your angels finally catch up, they find you in a heap of twisted metal, after your car ran off the road and crashed in a ditch.

Human beings are **inquisitive**. We want to understand everything that's happening to us while we are racing towards our self made goals. But what about God's purpose for our life? What about God's provision for us? What about God's hedge of protection, which is granted when we are under His wing, and within His will? What are the privileges that God gives us when he adopts us as His children? What are the mysteries that God solves for us when he tells His children a bedtime story? God wants us to cry out to Him in a relationship that can best be described as the relationship between a child and a father.

Jeremiah 33:2-3 NIV
[2] "This is what the Lord says, he who made the earth, the Lord who formed it and established it---the Lord is his name: [3] 'Call to me and I will answer you and tell you great and unsearchable things you do not know.'

The worship song that we sang at church today said, **"I lean not on my own understanding, my life is in the hand of the creator of heaven."** What does that song mean? Pastor Ken told us that we don't need to have all the answers, just trust in God. God put that **inquisitive spirit** in us, and he gave us free will so that would be better company for Him——better than the robotic angels, better than the stupid plants, dumb animals, and yucky insects. However, we don't need to have all the answers, or know the best path forward.

Think of a father who is trying to guide his five-year-old son across a busy intersection. The son has an impulse to run across the street without holding his father's hand, but the father restrains his son with a firm, yet loving grip. The son permits his father to take away his freedom, at least temporarily, so that the will of the father is done and the child's life is saved.

The son knows that he is loved by the father, and so he does not need to know about the physics involving his impact with the oncoming tractor trailer truck. Even if the five-year-old child was a genius, and he could understand the equations of momentum, the law of relativity, and the law of gravity–– that knowledge would not grant him the freedom of trying to out run a tractor trailer. The only thing that saves the boy is his loving relationship with his father, and the gentle, yet firm, tug by his father's hand on his shoulder. It is better to have a loving relationship with your father then it is to be a dead genius.

Similarly, for the child of God, the burdens of life are no longer on our shoulders, but rather at the feet of Jesus Christ. Yes, in the unimportant stuff, life is a chess game for us to master; but in the most important issue, our salvation, we don't have to figure it out for ourselves, because God already did the heavy lifting, and the heavy thinking. The answer was to send Jesus. God equipped Jesus with a human body, complete with flesh that bleeds and a free will which led Jesus to wonder if there was some way to avoid crucifixion–– but in the end he said, "Lord, let your will be done, not mine."

Jesus is part of the Holy Trinity. Jesus is fully God and fully man. Jesus is our King, yet he is also our brother, and he is an example of how Father God intends for us to live in a perfect relationship with Him. Why did Father God have to send a man, and not an angel, to secure our salvation? Simple answer: if God had sent an angel to die on the cross for our salvation, then people would shrug their shoulders and say, "we can't be that good, not as good as an angel." An angel could never be a good example for the correct use of our free will; nor could an angel have a perfect relationship, not a robotic relationship, with God.

So what are we to do? How are we to live according to God's good and perfect plan for us? We can't think our way into paradise, nor can we get to heaven by making all the right choices. No one can totally avoid sin. Jesus said that all we have to do is have faith like a child.

Innocent, child like faith removes the burden of sin and overthinking. Faith is the prerequisite for us to be called "children of God."

Luke 18:16-17 NIV

[16] But Jesus called the children to him and said, "Let the little children come to me, and do not hinder them, for the kingdom of God belongs to such as these. [17] Truly I tell you, anyone who will not receive the kingdom of God like a little child will never enter it."

It is good to be a ***child of God***, just as it is to be the child of a king. A prince or princess has privileges that the king bestows upon them. No ordinary person shares these privileges with the king's children. I share a bag of potato chips with my grandchildren, not with some random kids that I see playing in the shopping mall. It would just be wrong for me to offer potato chips to some random children who I do not have a relationship with, and I'm sure their mothers would take offense by my action, and call the police.

Some Christians ***lack faith***, and they live beneath the privilege that God intended for them to have. These Christians, lack a relationship with God. Jesus said, "you have not because you ask not." God won't give them the potato chips because they won't ask for some with faith.

Other Christians have an ***immature faith***, and God doesn't answer their prayers because they would start worshiping the gift instead of God, who is the giver of the gift. God is more concerned with our relationship with Him than he is with our gifting. The mature Christian will exhibit faith, even in times of hardship; and will offer to God praise, even during times of sadness.

Sometimes we try to put God in a box. "If I pray like this, then God will answer my prayers like that." God already knows what is in our hearts, and in our minds, and in our prayers. God created prayer so that we could talk to Him, as we go on a lifelong journey with Him. He does not need our advise, or for us to tell Him what we need. God honors our relationship throughout our walk with Him. Our faith matures with time and through hard lessons from life. The only reason God wants to hear your prayers is because He loves you, as He walks with you for all of your days. ***God cannot be manipulated, but he can be loved!*** He wants to hear your voice because he cherishes having a relationship with you. You are his child.

God is interested in our availability, not our ability. God does not call the equipped, but He equips those He calls. We must walk with Him as we putter around this earth. Although we have our own talents, all we really bring to the table is our faith, our obedience, our humility, and yes, of course, our love.

Jeremiah 29:11-13 NIV

[11] For I know the plans I have for you," declares the Lord, "plans to prosper you and not to harm you, plans to give you hope and a future. [12] Then you will call on me and come and pray to me, and I will listen to you. [13] You will seek me and find me when you seek me with all your heart.

Before the fall from the garden of Eden, Adam and Eve would take long, wonderful walks with God in the coolness of the morning, and their relationship with the Lord was perfect. But people never leave well enough alone, as we are not content to just walk with God. We forget that our hearts are a temple for the Holy Spirit——the heart is the house of the Lord.

Haggai 1:7-9 NIV

[7] This is what the Lord Almighty says: "Give careful thought to your ways. [8] Go up into the mountains and bring down timber and build my house, so that I may take pleasure in it and be honored, " says the Lord. [9] "You expected much, but see, it turned out to be little. What you brought home, I blew away. Why?" declares the Lord Almighty. "Because of my house, which remains a ruin, while each of you is busy with your own house.

The greatest mission is to raise good children and grandchildren, but you cannot teach what you do not know. If your mission only serves you, and not your family, and not your God, don't be surprised if your mission fails; on the other hand, God will grant you success if your put serving the kingdom of God as your primary goal, and raising your family a secondary goal.

Matthew 6:33-34 NIV

[33] But seek first his kingdom and his righteousness, and all these things will be given to you as well. [34] Therefore do not worry about tomorrow, for tomorrow will worry about itself. Each day has enough trouble of its own.

God owns the mansion on the hill, and you only own the tiny sandcastle on the beach. Without God, you are the king of a very small kingdom, a kingdom of one, and your sandcastle will be washed away with the next incoming tide. God, on the other hand, is the purveyor of the eternal kingdom of heaven. If you honor God's kingdom, then not only will He grant you eternal life, but He will also honor your little temporary kingdom on earth.

If you become a sweeper in the mansion that belongs to God, then God will adopt you as a child of His. God will come, like the good father, who brings a plastic shovel and pail to the beach, where his child is building a sandcastle. God honors what is important to you if you honor what is important to Him, and He will help you in your insignificant calling, as long as you seek first the kingdom of God and take part in His higher calling. You find God's purpose for your life when you seek first His kingdom.

Psalm 84:10 NIV

[10] Better is one day in your courts than a thousand elsewhere; I would rather be a doorkeeper in the house of my God than dwell in the tents of the wicked.

Elsayed: I thought this essay was great! Just finished reading! "Jesus said that all we have to do is have faith like a child. Innocent, child like faith removes the burden of sin and overthinking." How do we get back to that innocent faith you think?

Abdullah: Jesus said we have to be born again.

Elsayed: After our physical birth, why do we have to be 'born again?'

Abdullah: Nicodemus, a Jewish Pharisee, asked Jesus the same question. God cannot answer your questions if you don't have a peaceful, quiet heart. There are some questions that would be harmful for you to know the answer of, such as the exact year, day, time of your death.

What good would it be for you to know when you were going to die? We binge feed on useless/harmful information, and it's getting worse with the computer age, semiconductors, and the Internet. Sometimes it is better to be quiet and listen to God.

John 3:4 NIV

[4] "How can someone be born when they are old?" Nicodemus asked. "Surely they cannot enter a second time into their mother's womb to be born!"

Elsayed: Why are we here? What's our purpose? Is it because God condemned Adam?

Abdullah: The short answer is that our sole purpose is to glorify God. That is our only purpose. We are to glorify God, utilizing our free will; unlike the angels, who also glorify God, but do so robotically, because they have no free will outside of God's will.

Our free will makes it possible to rise above the angels, but it can also make us sink below the animals, if we misuse it. Animals have instinct, they kill to eat; but humans, with our free will, kill for sport; and angels only kill if it is God's will.

Adam and Eve had their chance to stay in paradise and enjoy a perfect relationship with God. However, sin intervened and God had to separate himself from his human creation. Jesus felt this separation, due to the sin of all humanity, when he was on the cross and asked God "why have you forsaken me?"

The worst thing that can happen to a human being is separation from God, and the best thing that can happen to a human being is reconciliation with God. Jesus made a path for us to be reconciled with God despite our sin.

Questioning God versus Being Quiet Before God.

"Who am I?" "What is the meaning of life?" "Is there life on Mars?"

We ask God a lot of inane questions, but then we don't even stick around to hear the answer. If I were God, I would tell the whole world, "just shut up and walk with me! I will tell you what you need to know, when you need to know it, but only if you need to know it, because too much knowledge is not good for you----remember the tree of the knowledge of good and evil? How is that working out for you? You think you are so smart! When Adam and Eve ate the fruit, they certainly bit off more knowledge than they could chew."

In the microwaveable, disposable, video game era in which we live, we don't **have the patience** to meditate on the word of God, or **the will** to pray to God, or **the quietness** to listen to the small still voice of God from within. In *Jeremiah 33:3*, God invites us to cry out to him, and he promises to give us answers to questions which we did not even have the wisdom to ask. In *Joshua 1:8*, we are advised to meditate on the word of God, day and night. In **Romans 10:9,** we are given the formula for salvation: **listen** to the word of God with your ears, **believe** the word with your heart, and **confess** with your mouth that Jesus Christ is who he said he was. Only then will your sins be exchanged for the righteousness of Jesus, and you will be reconciled with God.

Jeremiah 33:3 NIV

[3] 'Call to me and I will answer you and tell you great and unsearchable things you do not know.'

Joshua 1:8 NIV

[8] Keep this Book of the Law always on your lips; meditate on it day and night, so that you may be careful to do everything written in it. Then you will be prosperous and successful.

Romans 10:9-10 NIV

[9] If you declare with your mouth, "Jesus is Lord," and believe in your heart that God raised him from the dead, you will be saved. [10] For it is with your heart that you believe and are justified [made righteous before God], and it is with your mouth that you profess your faith and are saved [receive salvation].

Elsayed: What is the benefit of the second birth?

Abdullah: We all need a new beginning, a new spiritual birth. Whenever someone feels powerless to change a bad habit, a genetic predisposition, or an ancestral curse, we can press the reset button that only Jesus provides. With the reset button pressed, we can now obtain a new birth, free from the burden of past sin, and a new destiny.

Have you ever heard an alcoholic say, "I was just born that way," or a homosexual say, "I am genetically homosexual," or a short tempered person say, "I am Italian, all of my people have a tendency to be emotional."

Rather than blame their genetics, their culture, or perhaps the original sin of Adam and Eve, each one of these people need to be born again in the spirit, and to do that they must have faith like a child. Innocent, humble, child-like faith that removes the burden of sin and overthinking.

The good news is that we no longer have to hold ourselves up by our bootstraps. We no longer have to commit to our past sins and even our ancestral sins. With Jesus as our brother, we can go home to be adopted by his father, and become children of God. A child depends on his relationship with his father, who he knows will protect and provide for him, solely because of the father's love.

2 Corinthians 5:17-19 NIV

[17] Therefore, if anyone is in Christ, the new creation has come: The old has gone, the new is here! [18] All this is from God, who reconciled us to himself through Christ and gave us the ministry of reconciliation: [19] that God was reconciling the world to himself in Christ, not counting people's sins against them. And he has committed to us the message of reconciliation.

Elsayed: Give me an example of how we are 'born again.'

Abdullah: Jesus used parables to explain things; therefore I will give you the 'parable of the screen door.'

The Parable of the Screen Door.

Last weekend we did a father and son project of putting up a screen door. It took us about three hours to remove the old screen door and to replace it with the new one. I thought we were done, but then I realized that we had put the door knob assembly upside down and the latch was not properly engaging the door jamb. I told my son not to worry, he could go about his day, and take his wife and kids to the park. I was confident that I could fix the door knob without his help. It should only take me five minutes, right?

Wrong! What I didn't realize is that sin was about to enter into my project. The screen door was originally born out of a cardboard box that came from Lowe's. The door was not of a solid construction; instead, it was hollow, that is because it was made with the ancestral sin of greed from the manufacturer. Satan's deception is always based on hollow promises. It wasn't my fault that the door was hollow, I didn't make it, but this feature was about to change my whole afternoon.

As I unscrewed the door knob, to my horror, some of the parts fell inside the hollow center of the door. Frustrated, I didn't know what I should do. Should I order another door knob assembly, which would take three weeks to come by mail? No, I decided that I would not give up on the parts that fell inside the hollow door. I thought to myself, "Jesus wouldn't give up on our lost parts, he would come looking for the one lost sheep!"

The screen door project was in need of being 'born again.' To do the job right I had to undo all the hinges and struggle to remove the door from its comfortable rest, and then proceed to turn it upside down and shake it. I didn't stop shaking I until the door handle parts came out through the narrow opening.

After retrieving the stranded parts I was able to fix the door handle, put the door back on the hinges, and I made sure that the latch properly engaged with the door jamb.

Reconciliation with God makes it possible to be reconciled with all other relationships——the latch properly engages with the door jamb. Two hours later the problem was solved, and the screen door was 'born again!'

Luke 15:4 NIV

[4] "Suppose one of you has a hundred sheep and loses one of them. Doesn't he leave the ninety-nine in the open country and go after the lost sheep until he finds it?

Elsayed: Is there a judgement day for Christians as well? How do Christians repent after they've sinned and already became baptized?

Abdullah: Yes, Christians believe in the day of judgment. But I think the question you're really asking is, do Christians believe that Salvation gives them a license to live in sin? Although, our salvation does not depend on our deeds, the Christian will not sin because he fears that it will grieve God. Again, think of the child and his father. If a child loves his father then he will not want to grieve his father; he will do what his father says simply because he wants to hear the words, "well done my good and faithful servant." Those are the words that God will speak to us when we stand at the threshold of heaven. The following scripture is an account, in the words of Jesus himself, of the day of judgment:

Luke 21:25-36 NIV

[25] "There will be signs in the sun, moon and stars. On the earth, nations will be in anguish and perplexity at the roaring and tossing of the sea. [26] People will faint from terror, apprehensive of what is coming on the world, for the heavenly bodies will be shaken. [27] At that time they will see the Son of Man coming in a cloud with power and great glory. [28] When these things begin to take place, stand up and lift up your heads, because your redemption is drawing near." [29] He told them this parable: "Look at the fig tree and all the trees. [30] When they sprout leaves, you can see for yourselves and know that summer is near. [31] Even so, when you see these things happening, you know that the kingdom of God is near. [32] "Truly I tell you, this generation will certainly not pass away until all these things have happened. [33] Heaven and earth will pass away, but my words will never pass away. [34] "Be careful, or your hearts will be weighed down with carousing, drunkenness and the anxieties of life, and that day will close on you suddenly like a trap. [35] For it

will come on all those who live on the face of the whole earth. [36] Be always on the watch, and pray that you may be able to escape all that is about to happen, and that you may be able to stand before the Son of Man."

Abdullah: Muslims go to Mecca for pilgrimage and the atonement of their sins, They also sacrifice goats and lambs for the atonement of their sins. I have never been to Mecca in my lifetime, and since becoming a Christian, I have stopped sacrificing animals to shed their blood for my sin. What have I replaced Mecca and the blood of animals with? How are my sins atoned?

I don't have to go anywhere, because wherever I am, God is here. My heart is the temple of the Holy Spirit. I have the word of God in my Bible, I have the blood of Jesus that was spilled for me and all sinners, once and for all, for everyone who is ever created by God Almighty. I don't sacrifice bovine animals, but I do occasionally enjoy a cheeseburger at McDonald's.

During the pandemic my pastor said to us that even if the church is closed physically, it does not mean that it is closed spiritually. This is because every believers heart is the church. Our hearts are the temple of the Holy Spirit of God. We cannot be separated from the Love of God, because God lives in us, and he does His miraculous work through us.

Elsayed: So what's the process of being 'born again?' So is everyone born again through baptism?

Abdullah: Water baptism is physically important, but first we must be spirituality baptized by the Holy Spirit. The Holy Spirit baptism happens when you say with your mouth, and believe with your heart, that Jesus Christ is who he says he was: a savior to those who are sinful, lost, and overthinking their self-made destiny.

Chapter 5: The Holy Spirit.

Elsayed: Is the Holy Spirit God Himself?

Is He a separate entity? Or are Him, God, and Jesus one in the same?

Abdullah: The short answer——I am one person, yet I have a first, last, and a middle name; another example, the sun is one entity, yet it has light, mass, and heat. Hence, the Holy Spirit, God, and Jesus are three perspectives of the same being, which we call the Holy Trinity.

The identity of Jesus I will address elsewhere, but let us focus on the person of the Holy Spirit, and let's answer the age old question, "who is God, and how can we know him?"

Our perception of things depends on us using the appropriate corresponding sense. How do we perceive love? Not by our five senses. Mountains of poetry, and millions of love songs, cannot explain what love is. The reason why the Bible says "God is love," is to remind us that we cannot use any of our five senses to perceive his presence; it is only through our hearts that we can feel that God's love is near. Love is God's language, and the organ of perception is the human heart.

The Holy Spirit is like a fragrance that is carried by the wind. You can't see the wind but you know it's there because of the action that it takes when it blows a sailboat across the sea, or blows the hat off of a person who was walking down the street. Similarly, you can't see a fragrance, but anyone who goes into the bathroom after I've been in it will know that I was there! I left my fragrance behind. I don't want to sound blasphemous, but we know God was here because of His fragrance, the Holy Spirit, was left behind. And look, he left the seat up again! ——the seat joke pertains to me, not God! No blasphemy here.

I heard someone once say, "Jesus is my plunger, who keeps it moving, when sin clogs my pipes." Ok, that's blasphemous, but I heard that from a janitor friend who had just come to know the Lord, and he had us all rolling in laughter when he said, "Jesus is my plunger," at a men's retreat.

Do you remember, in your earliest childhood memories, how your grandmother smelled? I am 60 years old now and I can still remember how my grandmother used to smell, from my earliest memories before the age of three. When I go to heaven, and find my grandmother there, I will feel her love because that fragrance will be apparent, long before I ever see her with my eyes. The Holy Spirit is like that fragrance, it is the fragrance of love. It is the fragrance of someone you love, and it gives you comfort beyond your understanding.

I have five granddaughters and one grandson. Whenever Aubrey, my oldest granddaughter, hears me singing Christian hymns, in my deep baritone voice, she comes running to me, shouting, "grandpa is in the Spirit! Grandpa is in the Spirit!" She knows, at her tender age, that the Holy Spirit is near when grandpa bellows out a "God song."

How does my seven-year-old granddaughter know that I am "in the Spirit?" It is because she has developed her heart to know the things of God. Here is an essay about a grandson who smells the fragrance of his grandfather and finds peace. It is called, "his grandpa's shirt."

Elsayed: What is the Holy Spirit?

Abdullah: The Holy Spirit is like the earliest memory of the fragrance of someone you love. Smelling this makes you know that they are near. Let me explain with another parable.

His Grandpa's Shirt

Jesus said that it is good to have 'faith like a child.' How can we gauge the faith of a little child? How can we, as adults, recapture this faith?

Nolan was not your average one-and-a-half-year old boy. He was ahead of his years in a lot of ways, but in his strong faith he was like all other children.

Nolan could ride his dog, a Labrador retriever, like a horse. He would take his doggy to the park and, instead of going on the slide or the swings, he would dance to win the hearts of the girls, some of them were teenagers.

At my barbecue party Nolan surprised us all. Nolan refused to eat baby food and bland noodles, choosing instead to eat tandoori chicken with a side of vindaloo achar. He didn't even need milk to douse the heat on his tongue.

Both of Nolan's parents work, so quite often Nolan's grandparents would take care of him. From a child's perspective the love of a grandparent is better than that of a parent; those old folks let a kid get away with almost anything.

Nolan's grandpa happens to be my buddy, Gordon. Gordon is a retired Bronx police officer, he is as tough as nails, but he is very tender with his grandson. Grandpa Gordon revels at giving new experiences to Nolan. He taught Nolan to drink from a sippy cup instead of a bottle, and Nolan taught grandpa to play catch by throwing the sippy cup at him when the milk was all gone. Gordon made a nifty left handed catch, to which Nolan nonchalantly said, "nice catch, grandpa."

Gordon initiated Nolan into manhood by teaching Nolan to pee while standing up. Together they would pee, and they would play 'sink the battleship,' drowning the toilet paper with two fountains of urine. Nolan said, "hey grandpa, why are you peeing so slow? You didn't sink your side of the battleship. I'm not proud of you!"

At the end of the day, when it was long past bed time, Nolan fell asleep in front of the TV, on top of Gordon's chest. Gordon was also asleep, but when he woke up at two in the morning, he knew he had to put Nolan to bed without waking him.

The room was dark and very quiet, every sound was magnified. Each time Gordon tried to get up, or even tried to twist, Nolan started to whimper. Putting Nolan to bed was going to be a big challenge.

With great care, Gordon finally got up out off the sofa, with Nolan cradled in his arms. But just as Gordon started to walk across the living room Nolan woke up startled, crying out in the darkness, "grandpa, grandpa!"

Gordon didn't know exactly what to do. He stood motionless in the living room, but Nolan was now fully awake. Nolan couldn't see Gordon, nor could he hear him, but there was something about Gordon's strong arms and his presence that would make Nolan go right back to sleep. Gordon spoke softly, but clearly, these simple words to his grandson, "Nolan I'm here. Grandpa is here."

The little guy snapped right back to sleep. Although Nolan knew that he was small and weak, he knew that he had a champion who loved him through any depth of darkness. He knew the safest place in the whole world was to be in the loving, strong arms of his grandpa. Nolan could do many things, yet he was humble enough to know that, especially when the darkness comes, it's good to have faith in someone who's bigger than you.

Nolan had, "faith like a child."

Gordon could now easily put Nolan to bed. But what if he woke up again? Gordon had another idea. It had been a warm summers day and covering Nolan with a blanket was not necessary; instead, Gordon began to take off his shirt and proceeded to cover Nolan with it. This way, even if Nolan started to wake up, he would smell his grandfather's scent and go back to sleep.

Throughout the night Nolan would gain comfort from the scent of his grandfather's shirt. That shirt would give him the feeling that his grandpa is near. Perhaps grandpa's shirt was Nolan's first experience of the Holy Spirit.

As adults, how can we recapture this 'faith like a child?' At what point do we lose this faith? When do we lose our innocence? Our society puts a high value on independence. Children like to think of themselves as being self made by the age of eighteen, never looking back over their shoulder at the parents that raised them. And then there are the elderly, who are placed in nursing homes, never having the opportunity to interact with their grandchildren. Thank God for grandparents like Gordon and his wife, Anita.

God sends the Holy Spirit to answer our prayers in five ways:

1) through a small still voice within you.

2) through your dreams and visions.

3) through Scripture.

4) through people and angels that he sends for your help.

5) and through circumstances by which he opens one door and closes another, in order to bring you where he wants you to be.

When the disciples learned of Jesus' pending death, they asked him, "what should we do, master?"

Jesus responded by saying two things. First, he gave them the edict, "love one another." Second, he told them that "a comforter," the Holy Spirit, was coming to be with them even after Jesus was gone from this earth.

The Holy Spirit calls out to us through the darkness. Sometimes he whispers, sometimes he cries out in a firm, loud voice, "I am here! I am here!"

Elsayed: So baptism with the Holy Spirit is something that is more so felt within and not so much something that is recited?

Abdullah: Almost correct. You don't need to be in the presence of any other person to receive your salvation; however, there is a link between your spoken words, your ears, your brain, and your heart. When you say out loud "Jesus I need you in my life," it means that you have completed the circuit, from words, ears, brain, and heart.

Elsayed: Oh okay, I understand! At first I thought it was similar to the Shahada in Islam but this is different! The Shahada requires witnesses.

Abdullah: Becoming born again is a simple process, a process that is both recited and heartfelt. However, you don't need any witness to do this process. It is between you and God alone.

Elsayed: But don't I need the blessings from a priest?

Abdullah: No. Not at all. For all I know, as you are reading this text, you may have already become born again, if you believe with your heart and you recite with your words, "I am a sinner in need of a Savior. Jesus please come into my life."

I'll call you at 1 PM today to see if you're still at Muslim, or not!

Elsayed: Hah hah, sounds good!

Abdullah: Did you just laugh, Ha Hah Hah, or were you trying to say Hallelujah?

Elsayed: might be a little of both!

Text ended. After a brief prayer for him, I called my friend, Elsayed, promptly at 1PM.

Abdullah: Well, are you a Christian, or what?

Elsayed: Yes, I think so. But I don't feel any different.

Abdullah: Don't think! Don't feel! Just let yourself rejoice with the angels. The angels are celebrating your excellent choice!

Elsayed: I am confused, but happy! Why am I happy?

Abdullah: Because now you are a child of God. This is your birthday, and along with the angels, we're having a birthday party!

Jesus's First Miracle, and my Folly.

Soon after becoming a Christian, I was trying to impress a group of pastors at a prayer breakfast, saying, "I really love the first miracle of Jesus, the one where he turned water into wine, because it reminds me that I'm not a Muslim anymore whenever I drink, as Muslims don't drink alcohol!"

The pastors at my table started giving me strange looks, so I sought to redeem myself, saying, "It's not what you think. I drink to remind myself that I am no longer a Muslim. I often do my evangelizing at the local pub, where I meet other like-minded people who celebrate Jesus's first miracle."

By now, pastor Carl was about to say something, but before he could rebuke me, I continued to dig myself a deeper grave, saying, "but I don't drink the hard stuff----mostly I like the 'girly drinks,' preferably with a little paper umbrella, so that I can get in touch with my feminine side, and stand up for women's rights!" I was trying to be politically correct.

John 2:11 NIV

[11] What Jesus did here in Cana of Galilee was the first of the signs [turning water into wine] through which he revealed his glory; and his disciples believed in him.

Elsayed: Christians seem to always have more fun than Muslims and Jews. And then there is bacon, so delicious! But seriously, with so many deep conflicts happening around the world (Palestinian Israeli conflict and Afghanistan), and if God is a part of our family, why does He allow so many bad things to happen to so many people?

Abdullah: Although most Muslims are peaceful, a fanatical few have interpreted the language of the Koran as a command to kill the *'kafirs,'* usually Christians and Jews (kafir means infidel or unbeliever, or someone who does not believe in one *God and the day of judgment*). The terrorist's war against Christians and Jews is misguided even by the standard set by the Koran. This is because Christians and Jews are not atheists or polytheists; they do believe in *'one God and the day of judgment'*----there is no reason for Muslims to kill Christians and Jews on theological grounds, they are not *kafirs*. The Koran says that if you meet a Christian or a Jew "you should try to outdo one another in good deeds," it does not say "*behead them.*" The Koran calls Christians and

Jews "the people of the book," worthy of partnership, theological discussions, and spiritual exploration.

What is the history of *radical, Islamic terrorism*? War between rival Arab tribes was a fact of life during early Islam, and this is reflected in the writings of the Koran. For thousands of years the Middle East has been a cesspool for wars between Arab tribes, it would be wise for our politicians not to pick sides. In modern times, the Muslim's theological battle against non-Muslim Arab tribes have been replaced by a battle against Christians and Jews. Christians and Jews provide the usual target for a holy war, or jihad; but other Muslim 'tribes' have served as targets, particularly if they do not believe in the exact same version of Islam, as does the jihadist. These violent scriptures of the Koran are not transferable to modern times:

Sura 33, vs 61: they shall have a curse on them, and wherever they are found, they shall be seized and slain without mercy.

Sura 9, vs 29: slay those who believe in neither Allah or the last day.

Sura 22, vs 39: to those against whole war is made, permission is given to slay, because they are wrong and verily Allah is most powerful for your aid.

So why does God permit radical, Islamic terrorism? I would like to give a Christian overview of why God permits all suffering, and even terrorism. Here are three points: *first*, God honors the free will of man, including the terrorists will to bring death and distraction. Atheists will say that terrorism proves that God does not exist. A 'good God' would not have permitted terrorism if God really existed. Which leads me to my ***second*** point, God permitted terrorism to draw Believers to seek Him----persecution strengthens the church. Christianity in America has never been confronted with persecution until now. ***Third*** point: in the end God always wins. Now let's expand on these three points.

The apostle Paul writes in ***2Corinthians 12:10***, "that is why, for Christ's sake, I delight in weaknesses, and insults, and hardships, in persecutions, and difficulties. For when I am weak, then I am strong, because God's power is made perfect in weakness. " Ask any persecuted Christian missionary serving around the world, and he will say, "in the moment of our greatest suffering, we develop clarity to our vision so that we can plainly see God." Strangely, it seems that God is closest to us when we are in despair, and with our backs up against a wall.

Sometimes we even have to suffer at the hands of mortals to feel the fullness of God's presence: **_with great burden comes greater love_**. Survivors of 9/11 saw visions of Jesus in the stairwell; and as a sign of his presence, there was the amazing steel girders fashioned into a cross by the intense heat from the fire. God's love never forsakes us.

In the end God always wins. God has allowed Satan to have temporary dominion over the earth. Revelation 12:12 proclaims, "woe to the earth and sea, because the devil has gone down to you! He is filled with fury, because he knows that his time is short." Terrorists have prostituted themselves to Satan, but rest assured, God can take the most horrific deed spawned by Satan, turn it upside down, and use it to destroy the forces of evil from within. God uses evil to cannibalize evil. The very people opposed to God are used as tools to execute God's will.

Revelation 17:8-17 says, "the beast and the 10 horns you saw will hate the prostitute; they will bring her to ruin and leave her naked; they will eat her flash and burn her with fire. For God has put it into their hearts to accomplish His purpose by agreeing to give the beast their power to rule, until God's words are fulfilled."

There is solidarity with those who are suffering----I was once just a Muslim from Pakistan, but after 9/11, I have become a Christian from Manhattan Island. I could also relate with women and girls who suffer in Afghanistan under the Taliban rule.

I pray that God will invert the original purpose of this Satanic terrorist attack, and as such, God will bring more people to become seekers of His love. When times are good, we Americans think that our success comes from our own wisdom and might. Persecution reminds us that we are still vulnerable and need to turn to God for protection and answers. Furthermore, we need to pray for those who persecute us, just as Jesus prayed for his tormentors when he was on the cross. Despite 9/11, if we are motivated to pray and practice fasting, America can regain her spiritual center of gravity, and many more Muslims can encounter the precious love of Jesus Christ.

Chapter 6: Courtship and Understanding Women.

Elsayed: now that I am reconciled with God through the Gospel and the sacrifice of Jesus, I want to be reconciled with my Jewish girlfriend. Should I marry her?

Abdullah: You really are a handful for any councilor! Next, you'll ask me to put a man on the moon!

You have to be equally yoked with anyone you marry—— same religion for both of you. That means that both of you need to be Christians, in order for you to have a successful marriage. That being said, my wife and I first became Muslims, before we both became Christians 14 years into our marriage. She should have made me a Christian on day one, instead of converting to Islam. I need to hold that over her head more often!

You both have to be unselfish, and always seeking to anticipate one another's needs. As a man, you have to love your wife as Jesus loved the church, and he died for the church! But this is a conversation for another time, I will send you more parables on marriage: *'the parable of the peristalsis,'* no, I mean, *'the parable of the pedestal.'*

Elsayed: Kids with big noses aside, what about that whole Jew-Arab thing as a cause for friction?

Abdullah: What is the solution to the conflict in the Middle East? No problem, I got this.

I figured it out during a wedding of a Jewish friend of mine. It is this: there should be a law that forces Israelis to go to the weddings of Palestinians, and vice versa. The Palestinians would be required to leave their exploding tuxedos at the door, but just imagine how beautiful and full of hope the bride would be on her special day, and everyone loves doing the chicken dance.

Imagine if hundreds of young Palestinians and Israelis, who met at such weddings, married and started having kids of their own——kids with extremely large noses. That would really screw up the hateful theology of politicians on both sides. Imagine the awkwardness of Ahmed, the would be suicide bomber, when he recognizes Aaron from the wedding he attended last month. What's he going to say? "Hey, aren't you Aaron from the Israeli wedding? Lovely bride! Any children?

No not yet? I'm sorry, but I have to blow us up now, okay?" That would be ridiculous.

Killing cannot happen when the parties involved are humanized to one another, such as through a wedding. And why limit this inter-marriage law to only Arabs and Jews? We should have a law that causes black people to marry white people, and Asians to marry everybody else! The result will be that everyone's children will look like everyone else's children, and it will be impossible to be a racist just by the color of somebody skin. And you'll have Asian kids dunking basketballs, and solving calculus equations. Was Jeremy Lin good at math?

Elsayed: That's deep. Jeremy Lin graduated from Harvard, he won a championship playing basketball with the Toronto Raptors, but he only warmed the bench, and I don't know if he was good at math, but he was an Asian who could definitely dunk a basketball.

I need to know the 'parable of peristalsis' and the 'parable of the pedestal.' You promised you would tell me.

Abdullah: Your salvation, middle-east peace, intermarriages, asian kids who can dunk basketballs, and now you expect me to teach you about peristalsis and pedestals? I'll tell you everything you want to know, but first tell me one thing, mister pharmaceutical representative. You sell a medicine called Relistor, which is for opiate related constipation. Correct?

The Parable of Peristalsis.

Peristalsis is the normal, rhythmical, smooth muscle contraction of the colon which is inhibited by opiate medications. The medicine you sell, Relistor, reverses the paralysis that opiate medications cause, and peristalsis is brought back to normal, and the bowel movement normalizes. No more constipation! Now, how does this relate to marriage?

If you studied my essay titled, 'shaken not stirred,' You will recall that a man who is confronted with an angry, nagging, fighting wife, will have to "take his lumps and keep it moving." A man does not have the luxury of staying on the pity pot for too long. Marriage is like the opiate of life, and to reverse the constipation we must take Relistor, which is like a reality check——It is the truth, and the truth shall set you free, and it will move your bowels. So just remember, when crap gets hard, we have a truth remedy to keep it moving. No more constipation!

Elsayed: Is that it? That's so lame! Okay, what's the 'parable of the pedestal?'

Abdullah: Let me try a little bit harder with the 'parable of the pedestal.'

The Parable of the Pedestal.

A wife wants a Chihuahua as her lapdog, a Pit-Bull as her protector, and a Great-Dane in the sack. My wife knows I'm the Big-Dog. Woof, Woof!

A wife wants her husband to protect her, provide for her, and put her on a pedestal.

Constructing the pedestal has to be according to exact specifications, like when the Jews constructed the Tabernacle of God. When a man is constructing a pedestal for his wife, he must make it very tall because she is very important; and he must make it very heavy so she cannot lift it up, and throw it at him, in a fit of rage. She might even enlist her chivalrous husband to pick up the pedestal, and at her instruction, position it over his own head, and then to drop it.

Elsayed: All right, that one was a little better. What else you got doc? What about sex? I was only kidding! Isn't sex off-limits to talk about in church?

Abdullah: Most pastors don't want to talk about sex because they don't want to expose women for being too lazy about it. This is especially problematic because 80% of the people who go to church are women, and if the pastor would talk about sex in a manner that held women accountable, then his church would be whittled down to only 20%, and he would basically be left with a men's group.

Did I ever tell you that my wife got me kicked out of a men's group? She would call my friends, telling them everything that was wrong with me, and she would give them instructions on what to tell me. They couldn't kick her out of the men's group because she wasn't a part of it, so they kicked me out instead! True story.

I've got a ***three part sermon series on sex***, because my South Bronx church, without walls, doesn't have to pay rent! I'm cool with just a men's group for the truth! Only my wife can get me kicked out. Here are some pictures of my wife, who is my obsession, and the reason why my brains have leaked out!

The Marriage Bed

Hebrews 13:4 NIV

[4] Marriage should be honored by all, and the marriage bed kept pure, for God will judge the adulterer and all the sexually immoral.

Hebrews 13:4 KJV

"Marriage is honourable in all, and the bed undefiled: but whoremongers and adulterers God will judge."

Introduction: who can claim to understand the differences between men and women, and the full sanctity of marriage?

I am not a celibate priest who lacks first hand marriage experience. I am not a pastor, afraid to alienate two-thirds of his church, who are women. If he preaches about submission, a pastor risks downsizing his church into a small men's group; especially if he preaches on the subject of submission as it is written in Ephesians 5:22-24. That is why this scripture is not often spoken about from the pulpit. But God has a sense of humor. God used someone with the last name of 'Abdullah' as a source to help pastors preach about the subject of marriage. No one cares if I blow it——I am not the pastor of the church, so the ladies do not have to leave in protest. God uses 'the foolish things of this world to confound the wise,' and I am plenty foolish. Just ask my wife.

I am just an average married man. I am a medical doctor to people of the South Bronx, NYC, and I am a convert to Christianity from Islam. I write these three essays at my own peril. I predict that some women will have a hard time accepting what is written here, but I back up everything with scriptural references and personal experience. Do not assume that I am biased against women simply because I am a man. Hear the message, and do not judge the messenger.

What gives me the credentials to write on the subject of marriage? Thirty-five years of marriage to one woman, the wife of my youth, the mother of my children, and the cause of the thirty-five lumps on my head, one for each year of marriage, like tree rings. My wife has the divorce lawyer's phone number on her speed-dial----but I am not a victim of divorce, this is only by the grace of God, and the principles described in this essay series.

One thing I have learned over the years, 'it is more important to be happy than it is to be right.' Winning is overrated. The kind of fight that can end your marriage is the kind of fight you win. Anyone can win a fight if they are willing to win at the cost of love and respect, like a bull in a china shop. Fights or serious arguments often enter into a different dimension from which they started. The new dimension is more volatile, very imaginative, and terribly personal. These kind of fights are, in other words, what sex should be. Why not make love instead of war?

World War II ended 75 years ago, but it never ended for Japan and Russia. These two countries never signed a peace treaty because Russia continues to occupy four northern Japanese islands. The Prime Minister of Japan, Shinzo Abe, told Russian President, Vladimir Putin, "if we just insist on our own justice, we can never reconcile with our enemies and end the war." That advice is good for Japanese diplomacy, as it is for husbands and wives when they go to war with each other.

Jesus told us to be unselfish, saying to his disciples, "the first shall be last, and the last shall be first." In fact, the entire ministry of Jesus Christ can be summarized in just one word---- reconciliation---- between God and sinners, and reconciliation between sinners and other sinners. Before you start listing the sins of your spouse, you should realize that you are also a sinner who is in need of a savior. But what if you are at the end of your rope, and you see your spouse as your enemy? Jesus commanded, "love thy enemy."

Let us take the worst case scenario: loving your enemy. Loving your enemy starts with listening to your enemy. Men often zone out when they hear their wife speak. Women listen, but they do not often hear the message; instead, they judge the messenger. Women have a certain bias, irrespective of what their husband has to say. It won't matter if her husband has the cure to AIDS, or the solution to stop world hunger, she's not listening. She knows him so well, what could he possibly say that she doesn't already know? My wife never reads my books or essays, except to chide me, and to remind me that I don't practice what I preach. My wife assumes that she already knows everything that I could possibly say and, in her view, none of it is very important.

This problem dates back to the garden of Eden. Eve failed to respect the words of her husband. Eve never believed Adam when he warned that God told them not to eat of the tree of knowledge. In Eve's mind, Adam must have misunderstood God, or so the serpent said. Eve focused on the messenger, Adam, and not the message. She would rather believe some slick, smooth, serpent——like the gawking guys at the gym, or the cat-calling construction workers, or the dapper dudes at the bar.

Instead of finding solutions, every wife is looking inside her husband's words to find some comments that make her feel more secure and loved. She is not listening for solutions, she wants to hear words that make her feel secure in her relationship with her man. More on building communication skills in Part 3 of this study called, *how can we make the Viagra man a better listener.* 'Part 2 of this study describes the **Biblical rules for sex**. Sex is *'the highway of life,'* which God intends for our procreation and for us to celebrate our oneness with our spouse, a mirror of the exclusive relationship we have with God----but Satan wants to use this same highway as a road to our destruction.

Part 1: God's Love, God's Hierarchy, and Our Submission---- Somebody Tell a Feminist that Submission is Not a Dirty Word.

God's love, God's hierarchy, and our submission.

There are three kinds of love described in the book of Ephesians: the love that God has for humanity, the love that Jesus had for the church, and the love that a man is supposed to have for his wife. These three loves are really one and the same, as all love ultimately comes from a single source----God.

1 John 4:8 NIV

[8] Whoever does not love does not know God, because God is love.

Ephesians 5:21 NIV

[21] Submit to one another out of reverence for Christ.

God's kingdom is an orderly kingdom, it has structure, and it has hierarchy. In a kingdom where there is hierarchy it is necessary that some must submit to some others. In God's hierarchical system, one person does not degrade or put down the other; but rather, all factions edify and lift up all others. Why should there be a hierarchical system that requires submission in the church, and in the marriage? This system is a safeguard against Satan. The hierarchy is designed to protect churches and marriages from hostile, divisive, accusatory, Satanic thoughts that are designed to destroy both a marriage and a church. God's hierarchy lays down the rules that officiate the inevitable power struggle between the sexes. The book of Ephesians describes two parallel hierarchies, whereby the church is to be submitted to Jesus, and the wife is to be submitted to the husband.

Ephesians 5:22-24 NIV

[22] Wives, submit yourselves to your own husbands as you do to the Lord. [23] For the husband is the head of the wife as Christ is the head of the church, his body, of which he is the Savior. [24] Now as the church submits to Christ, so also wives should submit to their husbands in everything.

There is one notable outlier of God's kingdom: Satan. Satan wants to be his own god, and he wants nothing to do with God's hierarchy, or the edification of humans. Satan would rather destroy us all by causing division in churches, marriages, families, neighborhoods, nations---- the whole world. The ministry of Jesus is to reconcile us to God and to one another, which is the opposite of the ministry of Satan, whose ministry is to divide us from God and from one another. Satan wants to divide those who God has called to walk together in agreement, particularly in the church, and in a marriage. ***Satan's original purpose is to kill people before they are even born; and since people are born through acts of sex, it follows that Satan wants to cause division in our marriages, and perversion in our sex lives.***

Revelation 12:4-5 NIV

[4] The dragon stood in front of the woman who was about to give birth, so that it might devour her child the moment he was born. [5] She gave birth to a son, a male child, who "will rule all the nations with an iron scepter." And her child was snatched up to God and to his throne.

Sex, in the purest sense, is a way to worship God; it is not a favor, or an entitlement between human beings.

A strong marriage begins with two individuals who first seek intimacy with God, and then seek intimacy with one another. Why seek a monogamous relationship? Because God is big on exclusivity. Just as God wants us to seek

Him above all other relationships, **God designed marriage as a mirror of the exclusive bond that we have with God.** Sex is a celebration of the covenant between two partners in a marriage as they become 'one flesh.' Marriage vows provide us with a hedge of protection when in 10, 20, or 30 years, life gets tough, and sexual temptation outside of marriage creates a real and present danger.

The devil wants to kill you and your children. Starting in the garden of Eden, Satan's original purpose has been to kill people; and people are born from acts of sex, no wonder Satan wants to cause death through our sex lives. Satan wants to take sex, which God intended for our good, and he wants to perverse it, turn it around, and use it for evil. Sexual frustration in marriage can open the door to the devil, leading to temptation from outside of marriage. People who are hurt and frustrated will hurt and frustrate other people; and hurt people will take unnecessary risks, throwing their own safety to the wind. Testosterone is the cause of all wars, male pattern baldness, and convertible automobiles driven by bald guys. Monthly changes in estrogen and progesterone cause all kinds of craziness in women.

Division leads to sexual frustration. Most wars and violent crimes are caused by men, often as a result of sexual frustration and anger caused by testosterone; on the other hand, women are more prone to the ill effects of estrogen and progesterone, resulting in anxiety and depression. Both sexes equally suffer from pride and arrogance. Aside from sexual temptation, Satan uses arrogance, anger, and anxiety to destroy the good and perfect plan that God has for us. Let us prevent Satan from causing our spiritual and physical death, and let us see marriage and sexuality as God does----God sees sex as an act of worship.

Matthew 19:5-6 NIV

[5] For this reason a man will leave his father and mother and be united to his wife, and the two will become one flesh. [6] So they are no longer two, but one flesh. Therefore what God has joined together, let no one separate."

God had a perfect plan for Adam and Eve in paradise, a plan that Satan hated.

The power struggle first began in the garden of Eden between three people: Adam, Eve, and Satan. We must take a moment to understand what happened on that fateful day when Satan convinced Eve to eat from the tree of knowledge. Some theologians describe Jesus as the second Adam, because Jesus reclaimed the spiritual authority that Adam had lost when he ate of the fruit; but Jesus is also the perfecter of all loving relationships. The blood of Jesus reconciled sinners to God, and husbands to wives.

When it was all over, Adam and Eve had fallen from God's grace, and there was a curse placed on Adam, and a two-part curse placed on Eve. Not too many Christians can tell you what was the second part of Eve's curse, because they don't talk much about it in church; but the second part of her curse is the root of all battles between men and women. Let us study Eve's curse.

From the beginning of time, Satan has tempted **men through their eyes**, as with pornography on a computer screen, and Satan has tempted women **through their ears**, as with a gigolo's insincere flattery, or a girlfriend's hateful gossip.

Satan tempted Eve through her ears when he challenged what Adam had said about the dangers of the forbidden fruit. Eve was only equipped with second hand information from Adam about the tree of knowledge, she did not have the benefit of hearing from God directly.

Furthermore, Eve did not routinely listen to Adam, so she was not impressed when Adam told her that God did not want them to eat the forbidden fruit. She must have assumed that Adam heard God incorrectly. Subsequently, the serpent had a chance to make his case against the word of God.

After Eve was tempted **through her ears**, we can only imagine how she convinced Adam, as she no doubt tempted him **through his eyes**. She probably gave Adam a lap dance, squashing his obedience to God with every successive bump, grind and gyration. They ate the fruit of the tree of knowledge and then, literally, there was hell to pay. God cursed Adam and Eve.

God cursed Adam, telling him that he would have to toil on the earth and, unlike his carefree, limitless life in paradise, nothing would come easily on earth, and one day he would die.

Mercifully, God gave Adam the tools he would need to prosper on earth. Adam was given Devine authority, coupled with Devine responsibility to protect and provide for himself and his family. **God gave Eve a two-part** *curse*. First, God warned her that she would have painful childbirth. The second part of Eve's curse threw a monkey wrench into all future relationships between men and women; in **Genesis chapter 3**, the second part of Eve's curse says, "she will desire her man's authority but he shall have dominion over her."

Genesis 3:16 NIV

[16] To the woman he said, "I will make your pains in childbearing very severe; with painful labor you will give birth to children. Your desire will be for your husband, and he will rule over you."

In plain Bronx speak, the woman's curse is that **she wants to be the man,** and the man's curse is that **he has to be the man**. Here is the situation: the man has to protect and provide for his family and all the while he has to fend off attempts by his woman when she desires to usurp his authority. Unfortunately for Adam, his curse puts him directly in harms way of Eve's curse; she covets his authority to make choices, but God still holds the man responsible when things go wrong----hence, the foundation for all battles between husbands and wives.

Adam gave up a lot----he got the girl but it cost him a rib, paradise, authority over all of the earth, and his immortal life. Can he get a refund?

Before there was a TV reality show called '*the bachelor in paradise*,' there was the garden of Eden, where Adam lived alone in a real paradise. Adam was made in the image of God. Adam had spiritual authority over the world, and he was commissioned by God to name all created beings. **Adam was self sufficient, but he was painfully alone.** So God saw it fit to give Adam a helpmate. Eve was born from a rib taken out of the side of Adam's body. Adam could not help but love her because she was, "bone of my bone, and flesh of my flesh." Adam's day job was to have dominion over the world; but his night job, his infatuation, was to love Eve. Loving Eve was not hard because she was a part of him, and Adam loved himself; but also, Eve had those 'baby friendly' parts that made Adam interested in procreation.

Adam forfeited bachelorhood in the garden of Eden in order to get married to Eve; but worse than that, by eating the forbidden fruit, Adam gave up the spiritual authority, that was originally granted to him by God, to Satan. But God had a plan to give the descendants of Adam and Eve a second chance. God sent Jesus to correct Adam's mistake. Jesus took that spiritual authority back from Satan and gave it to the church. Jesus loved the church the same way Adam loved his wife.

Jesus reclaimed the spiritual authority that Adam had foolishly lost; moreover, Jesus is the perfect example of a husband's love for his bride----Jesus died for the church----how many of us men would be willing to die spiritually, if not physically, for his wife? What if we just gave up the right to be right? What if we sought our wives version of justice instead of our own? Now this kind of 'death' is more difficult than merely throwing yourself in front of a bullet to save your wife.

Ephesians 5:25-33 NIV

[25] Husbands, love your wives, just as Christ loved the church and gave himself up for her [26] to make her holy, cleansing her by the washing with water through the word, [27] and to present her to himself as a radiant church, without stain or wrinkle or any other blemish, but holy and blameless. [28] In this same way, husbands ought to love their wives as their own bodies. He who loves his wife loves himself. [29] After all, no one ever hated their own body, but they feed and care for their body, just as Christ does the church--- [30] for we are members of his body. [31] "For this reason a man will leave his father and mother and be united to his wife, and the two will become one flesh." [32] This is a profound mystery---but I am talking about Christ and the church. [33] However, each one of you also must love his wife as he loves himself, and the wife must respect her husband.

There is a fine line between a woman who gives life to her man, and one who takes his life away.

Although men should be willing to die for their wives, as Christ died for the church; on the other hand, women should not be the one's who ask their men to die for them. ***As they say in the Bronx, "don't try to die for a woman who's trying to kill you."*** When a husband asks his wife, "am I making enough money to keep you comfortable?" The wife should respond by saying, "God is our ultimate provider and what I have from you is sufficient." She shouldn't say, "you need to make more money before I give you love and respect, you lazy bum!"

A good woman is a ray of light to guide her husband, so that he does not stumble; a bad woman is a destructive laser beam which burns right through him. A good woman is life giving water; a bad woman is the explosive separate gaseous components of water: hydrogen and oxygen. If the man is the head of the family, then a good woman is the neck that turns the head; a bad woman is the neck that chokes the head, starving his brain of oxygen.

What is a wife's Biblical responsibility? Wives are supposed to win their husbands over, not by words, but by the 'purity and reverence of their lives.' Some women say, "I will only submit to my husband only if he is fully submitted to God." That sounds right, but it is not----it is not scripturally correct to wait for perfection in a husband before a wife submits to him. She married and became 'one flesh' with her husband, so if he lacks spirituality, what should she do? ***The wife must pray for his spiritual growth, and she must lead by example: she must teach her husband how to submit to God, in a way that reflects how she is submitted to her husband.*** It is uncommon to find a woman who teaches by example, as most women are tremendously good talkers.

1 Peter 3:1-2 NIV

[1] Wives, in the same way submit yourselves to your own husbands so that, if any of them do not believe the word, they may be won over without words by the behavior of their wives, [2] when they see the purity and reverence of your live.

All marriage courts have a legalistic obsession with rules and regulations, an obsession that tries to circumvent God's grace and mercy. Legalistic approaches to a marriage and, for that matter, to a religion, become a reason to mistreat people, followed by a desire to have a theological debate, followed by divorce, followed by a desire to kill every opponent. To offset these legalistic tendencies, Jesus simply said, "love one another," and he went even further, by saying, "love thy enemy."

Jesus knew that within each and everyone of us, there is both a victim and a villain. Your enemy has struggles that are similar to your own; maybe, just maybe, your enemy is a greater victim then you, and you are a greater villain then he. We are all villains to some degree, but fortunately, God can use even a villain to fulfill His master plan. It is good to befriend a victim, but it is better to show empathy for a villain. One day, when we stand before God, we will all have to answer for having been the villain.

Jesus calls us to "love thy enemy." This edict takes away the burden of revenge, and it bridges the victim/villain inconsistency within our very own soul. Jesus displays the perfect model of reconciliation and healing. If you follow Jesus, you may suddenly find that your enemy is your friend, and your spouse is once again your lover and soulmate.

Submission----someone please tell a feminist that submission is not a dirty word.

Ephesians 5:22-24 NIV

[22] Wives, submit yourselves to your own husbands as you do to the Lord. [23] For the husband is the head of the wife as Christ is the head of the church, his body, of which he is the Savior. [24] Now as the church submits to Christ, so also wives should submit to their husbands in everything.

What is a married woman's submission to her husband supposed to look like? It is not described by daily foot massages at five o'clock in the morning, followed by breakfast in bed. When my wife submits to me it means that she is watching my back against the wiles of Satan. **When husband-and-wife are on the same page, Satan cannot put a wedge between them, and the couple can do great and mighty things to advance the kingdom of God.** Think of a police show on TV, two cops are fighting a bad guy. During the shoot out one cop says to the other, "I've got your back, "and the other cop proceeds forward to get a better position to fight the enemy. The submissive wife has 'her husband's back.'

Any successful CEO of a company will tell you that he listens carefully to the advice from the second in charge person. My wife through the years has offered her woman's intuition to help me deal with business partners, children, and all people I have encountered throughout my life. The more I listen to my wife, the more I become successful in my life. Happy wife, happy life.

But if mama ain't happy, nobody is happy, and then we have a lovers quarrel. That's not a big deal, as long as we 'do not let the sun go down on our anger,' as advised by the Bible.

Thirty-two years ago, I met my wife in the Bronx. She was Christian, and I was a Muslim. I persuaded her to become a Muslim so that she could marry me. She remained a Muslim for ten years, but then she returned to Christianity during a tumultuous period in our marriage. I did not want to interfere with her Christian faith, because I could see that it brought her great solace.

Furthermore, I was afraid that if I forced her to choose between her faith and me that she would say, "it's Yahweh, or the highway." My wife never gave me an ultimatum; instead, Jesus appeared to me in a dream as a result of my wife praying for me at 3 o'clock in the morning, every day, over three weeks. Ladies, please ***pray for your husbands***, it is the highest form of submission.

Feminist think that 'submission' is a dirty word, but the Bible calls married women to wear submission as if it was a beautiful dress, or a pretty hairstyle.

1 Peter 3:3-5 Your beauty should not come from outward adornment, such as elaborate hairstyles and the wearing of gold jewelry or fine clothes. Rather, it should be that of your inner self, the unfading beauty of a gentle and quiet spirit, which is of great worth in gods sight. For this is the way the holy women of the past who put their hope in God used to adorn themselves. They submitted themselves to their own husbands.

An interesting aside about fashion: a modern woman's fashion strategy is largely in response to a man's ***sex drive***. Remember that men are tempted through the eyes, and women are tempted through the ears. Women who dress immodestly are feeding into a man's sexual desire; they are demeaning themselves, in God's eyes, just to appeal to a man's base desires. High-heal shoes are the best example of a fashion design that makes a woman's legs look longer, while forcing her to stick out her butt, all the while causing her to nearly fall and break her ankles. She will have bunions when she is old, but by then men don't care because ***old women are invisible to a man's sex drive***.

Evil men do not care if old women suffer with bunions from the high-heal shoes. Men designed the high-heal----there is no self respecting woman who wants bunions when she is old. Of course, some women will say that they dress immodestly for themselves, or for other women, but we all know the real reason is so that they can attract the opposite sex. This lack of modesty is disgusting, and is demeaning to the dignity of women; yet feminists think it is more demeaning if a Christian woman submits to her husband.

The key for women is this: even though a married woman has to submit to her husband, she is wise to first find a man who is worthy of her submission. A good man will love his wife when she is young, and he will love her more, and massage her bunions, when she grows old. Don't marry an abuser, or a loser, because a husband is supposed to protect and provide for you and your family----that is the curse that befell Adam. Above all, make sure the man that you marry has a heart for the Lord. Although you have to submit to your husband, don't be submissive to just any man. You must make sure that he has already submitted himself to the Lord. Do not let love, sex, and hormones cloud your thinking. Ladies, don't marry someone who you think you can change, marry someone who has already changed into having a heart for the Lord. After you are married you must continuously pray for your man. This is because neither the devil, nor Jesus, are done influencing your man's life. A good woman tips the balance in favor of Jesus, and not the devil, through her prayers for her man.

Pastor Joyce Meyers gave a wonderful illustration about how the female eagle chooses her mate. The male eagle must pass her test before mating. She carries a stick to a high altitude and drops it, expecting the male to catch it before it hits the ground. If he drops it he will not be permitted to mate with her. To make matters more interesting, she flies to a lower and lower altitude, using progressively larger and larger sticks. The female eagle is more selective than most women are when they select a mate.

I am like that male eagle, but instead of catching branches, I clean pots and pans for my wife. This is a great way for me to subsequently get sex, but that is not my shallow reason for cleaning the pots and pans. I love my wife, and I love her cooking. She is more likely to cook a meal for me if she remembers that I cleaned the pots the last time she cooked. But there is another reason why I clean the pots. It is because I do not want her to get massive forearms from cleaning pots.

I am a man, and I have strong forearms—— that is how God made me. I like to use my strong arms for lifting heavy pots full of dirty dishwater so that my wife does not have to clean after she cooks. I grew up in a Muslim household where my father never lifted a finger in the kitchen to help my mother; subsequently, my four-foot-eleven mother had forearms the size of a male weightlifter. To this day I have memories of my mother easily moving heavy pots that I could not even lift as a young man. I do not want a wife who has massive forearms with a tattoo of an anchor on the veiny side. I do not want my wife's dainty forearms to grow into 'Popeye the sailor man' arms (Popeye is an old cartoon about a sailor who ate spinach for strength). My wife does not even eat spinach because it makes her constipated.

Part 2: The Biblical Rules for Sex----Rules of the Road for the 'Highway of Life.'

If the marriage bed is the car that takes us down the 'highway of life,' then adultery is like a high-speed crash on that highway, and celibacy despite being married is like running out of gas, or having a flat tire on the side of the road.

Sex is like taking a joy ride in a fast car, riding down the 'highway of life,' and the final destination is 'Babyville.' God intends for us to have pleasure while we procreate; sex helps us enjoy the ride, or else some people would never want to get into the car. Unfortunately, although the town of 'Babyville' is near the town of 'Wedlock,' there are too many babies born just outside of wedlock----that is, babies are born without the parents being married. These children sometimes never know their father.

Sex outside of marriage, or even pornography, is like driving aggressively down the 'highway of life' with someone you hardly know. You are drunk with the desire for more and more speed, without seatbelts (without the covenant of marriage), and your destination is never intended to be 'Babyville,' but instead, some sleazy, one-night-stand hotel, just outside of the town of 'Wedlock.'

You get used to driving 110 mph, in the left lane; and then driving 55 miles in the right lane, with your spouse, feels like it's way too slow, and not very interesting. Before marriage, the adulterer says, "why buy the cow when you can have the milk for free;" after marriage, the adulterer says, "why put up with my cow at all?----she 'moos' too much, and I have grown lactose intolerant!" The adulterer finds very little incentive to keep his marriage healthy and mutually fulfilling.

No one ever thinks that they will crash, speeding down the 'highway of life,' at least not until it happens. An adulterous crash on the 'highway of life' has terrible repercussions: a broken heart, a broken relationship with God, disease, divorce, and abortion, all of which lead to physical, spiritual, and emotional problems. You do not want to go down that road, because it is not God's best for you. God says marriage is honorable, the marriage bed is undefiled, and the marriage covenant is kept between two people individually with God, and with each other.

Christians will not travel on this 'highway of life' unless certain safeguards are in place: 1) we choose our traveling partner wisely, put on the seatbelt of marriage, and commit to stay together for life. 2) we follow the speed limit, waiting for maturity before we merge onto the 'highway of life.' 3) if we lose our map, and we get caught up in the joy ride, and we find ourselves in 'Babyville' sooner than expected----then we keep the baby----we do not get an abortion, as that would go against the whole purpose of the 'highway to life.'

Sex is a Celebration of being 'one flesh' with your spouse.

Let us focus on **1 Corinthians 7:3-5**. To paraphrase, in a marriage it is written that one partner cannot unilaterally refuse to have sex; the only concession would be if one or both people wanted to set aside time for prayer instead of having sex. Listen up, ladies. If one partner in a marriage wants sex, and both parties are able, then biblically, sex must happen. This is because God understands our sinful nature and our struggle with temptation for sex outside of the marriage.

1 Corinthians 7:3-5 NIV

[3] The husband should fulfill his marital duty to his wife, and likewise the wife to her husband. [4] The wife does not have authority over her own body but yields it to her husband. In the same way, the husband does not have authority over his own body but yields it to his wife. [5] Do not deprive each other except perhaps by mutual consent and for a time, so that you may devote yourselves to prayer. Then come together again so that Satan will not tempt you because of your lack of self-control.

For the past three weeks I have devoted myself to the Lord while writing my book; during this period I have abstained from watching TV, exercise, and even sex, all so that I could concentrate on the Lord. My wife and I have mutually decided that for three weeks we will abstain from sex. I want to abstain from sex until I finish writing this book for the Lord, and she wants to abstain because she hates me.

Just kidding, my wife really loves me. She got me a Cardiology newsletter because she really cares about my health. She wants to keep me alive, for good sport, so that she can kill me later. In a study that was quoted in the newsletter it said that cardiac health is improved if we have sex at least twice a week; furthermore, the incidence of prostate cancer is reduced if a man has sex at least five times a week. My fuzzy math tells me that for the best health a married couple should have sex seven days a week, but that never happens, and so men usually die before their wives because of a lack of sex.

If sex is the 'highway of life,' then celibacy for married men is like having a flat tire. He physically can't have sex.

The Bible is very clear, in 1 Corinthians 7:3-5, that sex must happen if just one person in a married couple wishes for it to happen. This does not give a husband the right to rape his wife, as the scripture, in Ephesians 5:25-33, tells a man to be exceedingly loving and kind to his wife, as Christ loved the church. Sex must happen for a kind and loving husband, barring some medical or psychological illness, or the immediate need for prayer----let us say, if an astroid was about hit earth; although, an asteroid would be a good reason for a final sex romp before we die.

What would be a medical or psychological reason for celibacy in a Christian marriage? If a man doesn't have sex it is because **he can't for physical reasons,** and if a woman doesn't have sex it is because **she won't for emotional** reasons. In a man, sometimes the 'tire is flat' for physical reasons, and you need Viagra so you can repair the tire, before getting back on the road.

My favorite Viagra commercial is the one where the guy is driving down the highway towing a trailer full of horses, and his truck gets stuck in the mud. But the Viagra man is completely rational, and he knows just what to do in times of adversity, despite the fact that he has erectile dysfunction. Sometimes I wish I had erectile dysfunction, just so that I could take Viagra and become exceedingly rational, like the heroic Viagra man!

The horses in the commercial are a convenient metaphor for the man's unfulfilled sexual desire. The Viagra man takes the horses out of the trailer and ties them to the front of the truck and pulls it out of the mud. Viagra gave him the wisdom to free his truck from the mud using horse power! The final scene of the commercial shows the Viagra man's truck, with the horses safely in the trailer, arriving at his home, where he is greeted by his wife, who has no clue about his erectile dysfunction, the Viagra, or his powerful sexual desire that is driven by horses. Maybe I need to go out and buy a horse, a truck, and some Viagra!

An empty emotional gas tank is the cause of celibacy in married women. She won't have sex because she doesn't want to.

Women don't get flat tires on the 'highway of life.' When a married woman wants to be celibate it's usually for emotional, not physical, reasons---- ***her emotional gas tank is empty, and the fuel gauge doesn't work. She will not tell him what is wrong.***

The good husband always makes sure his wife's emotional tank is full. Being that her fuel gauge is broken, the emotional tank must be topped off at every available gas station, or else the husband will have to push the car without any help from his wife, because it's all his fault if the car runs out of gas. It is also his fault if they get lost, because men never admit that they are lost, and they never stop to ask for directions.

But things can get worse, **what if there's a hole in the emotional gas tank and it leaks out for no rational reason?** What if there are too many hormones----PMS; or not enough hormones----menopause? What if she worries too much and never prays? ***If she prays then why worry, but if she worries then why pray?*** Anxiety can put a big hole in the emotional gas tank.

Married life comes with a host of simultaneous, yet predictable, problems: work, finances, and raising children, to name just a few. ***Some quick advice for raising children***: first you must be the parent, then you must become a coach, then you must become a friend, and then finally, you have to conspire to spend your children's inheritance before you die. **Let go of your children, and let God take care of them**. You can not plan out their lives, just as you can not plan out your own life. There's no sense in trying to 'cross the bridge before we get to it,' because there are too many bridges and not enough time, or resources; and there's no sense in waiting until tomorrow before we start enjoying life today---go on and retire, buy that recreational vehicle, and you and the misses go touring the country!

Matthew 6:34 NIV

A[34] Therefore do not worry about tomorrow, for tomorrow will worry about itself. Each day has enough trouble of its own.

Statistics have it that *one out of every four women* will suffer a major episode of anxiety, and/ or, depression; in contrast, *one out of every eleven men* will suffer from anxiety, and/or, depression during the course of life. Anxiety and fear for tomorrow will prevent a woman from enjoying life today; also a woman will hold onto guilt, shame and regret from the past. Jesus advised us not to chase after solving future problems; the future, with all of its problems, will come on it's own, and the past is unchangeable history.

1 Peter 5:6-7

So humble yourselves under the mighty power of God, and at the right time he will lift you up in honor. Give all your worries and cares to God, for he cares about you.

Some practical advice for wives: if your husband brings you flowers don't assume that he's done something wrong; if your husband complements you and is sexually attracted to you do not dismiss his advances. Do not let poor self-esteem, or anger, or anxiety, or boredom get in the way of receiving gifts from your husband. Do not tempt him to give those gifts to some other woman. **Some practical advice for husbands (from the gigolo's handbook)**: men who are good listeners get more sex than those who rationally tried to solve their wives problems---- women are tempted through the ears.

What does the Bible say about separation and divorce?

Does celibacy have a place in a Christian marriage? Is there any reason for a married couple, who the Bible says are of 'one flesh,' to go back to being two separate people? **Apparently, the only reason Jesus gives for a divorce is adultery**. You can't leave your wife because she has a few wrinkles, or because she burned your toast; you can't leave your husband because he has a potbelly, Hillbilly teeth, or because he lost his job.

Matthew 19:8-12 NIV

[8] Jesus replied, "Moses permitted you to divorce your wives because your hearts were hard. But it was not this way from the beginning. [9] I tell you that anyone who divorces his wife, except for sexual immorality, and marries another woman commits adultery." [10] The disciples said to him, "If this is the situation between a husband and wife, it is better not to marry." [11] Jesus replied, "Not everyone can accept this word, but only those to whom it has been given. [12] For there are eunuchs who were born that way, and there are eunuchs who have been made eunuchs by others---and there are those

who choose to live like eunuchs for the sake of the kingdom of heaven. The one who can accept this should accept it."

In the above scripture, ***Jesus recommends that a man should become "like a eunuch for the sake of the kingdom of heaven."*** That recommendation may be a little severe for most men, but the apostle Paul echoes this same sentiment. The apostle Paul never married, and on more than one occasion he recommends celibacy for those who want to seek the kingdom of God. But thankfully, we do not all need to be eunuchs, as the scriptures also say: ***if you can not defeat sexual temptation, then it is better for you to be married and stay faithful to just one spouse***, and remain married to the wife, or the husband, from your youth.

1 Corinthians 7:1-2 NIV
[1] Now for the matters you wrote about: "It is good for a man not to have sexual relations with a woman." [2] But since sexual immorality is occurring, each man should have sexual relations with his own wife, and each woman with her own husband.

1 Corinthians 7:8-11 NIV
[8] Now to the unmarried and the widows I say: It is good for them to stay unmarried, as I do. [9] But if they cannot control themselves, they should marry, for it is better to marry than to burn with passion. [10] To the married I give this command (not I, but the Lord): A wife must not separate from her husband. [11] But if she does, she must remain unmarried or else be reconciled to her husband. And a husband must not divorce his wife.

Proverbs 5:15-18 NIV
[15] Drink water from your own cistern, running water from your own well. [16] Should your springs overflow in the streets, your streams of water in the public squares? [17] Let them be yours alone, never to be shared with strangers. [18] May your fountain be blessed, and may you rejoice in the wife of your youth.

Malachi 2:14-15 NIV
[14] You ask, "Why?" It is because the Lord is the witness between you and the wife of your youth. You have been unfaithful to her, though she is your partner, the wife of your marriage covenant. [15] Has not the one God made you? You belong to him in body and spirit. And what does the one God seek? Godly offspring. So be on your guard, and do not be unfaithful to the wife of

your youth.

God created Adam and Eve, not Adam and Steve.

After marriage some men believe they must apologize for their rationality and masculinity, and promise to become more emotional, so as to be better companions for their wives. Women get along just fine with homosexual men, but these kind of men would rather take a drive down the 'highway of life' with another man, and they have no plans to visit 'Babyville.' Incidentally, masturbation is also a sin because we never procreate, and we never get to 'Babyville,' as God intended.

Masturbation and Internet pornography do not result in oneness with one's spouse; masturbation is selfish and it was not part of God's plan for marriage because it does not reconcile us with our spouse, or lead to procreation. One of the old testament prophets showed his rebellion against God through masturbating: "he spilled his seed on the ground" instead of procreating with the wife God had ordained for him. ***Homosexuality is just a glorified form of masturbation; it is a sin, but no worse a sin than other forms of adultery.*** We should not be the one to 'throw the first stone' at a homosexual person because we are all guilty of sexual sin. Married people should never masturbate because it shows a lack of faith in the partner that was given by God; nor should married people deprive one another of sex, because sex is a celebration of being 'one flesh' with your spouse.

Genesis 38:9-10 NIV

[9] But Onan knew that the child would not be his; so whenever he slept with his brother's wife, he spilled his semen on the ground to keep from providing offspring for his brother. [10] What he did was wicked in the Lord's sight; so the Lord put him to death also.

Some women will tell you, "the most attractive men are homosexuals, or at least metrosexuals, but they aren't interested in women----too bad for me!"

These non-heterosexual men have feminine tendencies, and are more likely to know how to fill a woman's emotional tank than any heterosexual man. But one important question remains, ***"why can't a woman allow a heterosexual man to just be a man?"*** Wives must not purposely cause sexual frustration in their heterosexual men. Respect him and have sex when he asks for it. Testosterone mixed with sexual frustration causes men to participate in violent crimes, and sexually frustrated men tend to start wars with other nations, and bald men tend to drive around in convertibles.

A real man will protect and provide for his family, he won't listen to his wife's gossip, he will get bored, and occasionally he will scratch himself and smell his fingers while she is talking. **Real men** smell like the monkey cage at the zoo. Deal with it ladies, because the ***pretty boys*** may smell nice, and they get their body hair waxed, and eyebrows plucked, but they don't want you!

Besides homosexuality, what else goes against God's plan for 'the highway to life?' Let us make a list: abortion, premarital sex, divorce (if it is not due to adultery), feminism, masturbation, homosexuality (which is just a glorified form of masturbation)-----all of these have one thing in common: these all either prevent babies from being born, or destroy their families soon after they are born, or create so much sexual frustration that men are driven to war and other acts of violence. Remember, Satan's original purpose is to kill people by causing perversion in the marital bed. Godly sex is a form of worship, and a sign of a reconciled relationship; but perverse sex plays into the devil's schemes, and destroys our lives.

Jesus said, "the golden rule is to do onto to others as you would have others do you onto to you," but in relationships with our spouses we must follow the 'platinum rule,' which goes even further: ***"treat others as they would want to be treated----not necessarily the way you want to be treated."*** Personally, I would like to be treated with a Philly cheese steak hero, a cold beer, and an afternoon watching the ball game with my dog in my easy chair. I could gift my wife those same things, but I don't think she'd really like them. I highly recommend reading a book called, "the five love languages." This book helps us figure out how each person wants to be loved. Figure out how she wants to be loved and then love her that way. It sound so simple, but hormones make it complicated---either she has too much estrogen, or not enough; and the same can be said for men and testosterone----either we have too much testosterone when we are young bucks, or not enough when we are old reptiles, with 'a-reptile' dysfunction. Part 3 of the series will address ***'how to make the Viagra man a better listener.'***

Part 3: How can we make the Viagra man a Better Listener?

Husband, you cannot love your wife without listening to her.

I tested the title of this essay on some of the women in my Bible study, and one particularly staunch, nearly feminist, Indian sister at my Bible study had this to say about my title, "that's right! We need to make our men listen better. At all times they need to learn to listen better!"

Everyone at the Bible study had a roaring belly laugh, because it seems my Indian sister didn't understand the innuendo in this title. The Viagra man is a man of action and he is on a time clock. Having swallowed the little blue pill he only has four hours to please his wife. Meanwhile, his wife wants to talk for three hours and fifty-nine minutes, and she feels it is imperative for him to listen to every word. When he finally performs for her, lasting only one minute because the Viagra ran out, she will accuse him of not lasting long enough to please her!

True, men would be better listeners if women would talk less, and get to the point sooner; never the less, we men must learn the art of conversation. We must learn to sympathize and empathize with our wives. Empathy starts with an open ear, but there is a difference between just hearing and actually listening for feelings and fears.

Sometimes the words don't even matter; someone can say, "I'm just fine," but they way they say it, the body language, tells you that they are not fine, but they are really hurting inside. How many times have we said, "it's not what you're saying, but how you're saying it, that bothers me!" There is a deeper level to what we say. People respond more to our empathy, or lack of empathy, than to our words.

Romans 15:2

We must bear the burden of being considerate of the doubts and fears of others.

Paul McCartney, of the Beatles, said that the main reason for his band's success was this: "The songs were written to be about feelings between two lovers. The words were always about he and she, or I and you; for instance, 'with love from me to you', and, 'please me, like I please you.'" The songs were about feelings that people encounter when they are in love. The words never attempted to solve anyone's problems; if they had done that, then the songs would have never become so popular. The lyrics merely stated an emotional reality. It's no wonder that droves of teenage girls in the 1960s loved the Beatles and loved their songs. Looking back at Beatles songs today, I rekindle the fond emotions that I felt when I first listened to those carefree love songs as a young man. These were songs that offered no solutions to love, life, or anything else, but they left a mark on everyone's heart, both male and female. We remember the feelings, not necessarily the words.

Even after thirty-two years of marriage, I have trouble with these two things: listening to my wife, and reframing from providing a solution. Just the other day, I think she was telling me something about my being a poor listener, but I wasn't paying attention, so I don't know for sure.

Never the less, not knowing what she was saying, I proceeded to give her an answer to a question that I don't think she asked. I told her, "bowling balls! We need new bowling balls. " That made her more irate. I can't understand why. I didn't mean her any harm. I don't even know how to bowl.

What is going on here? A **woman** will carefully set up ten bowling pins of her problems, never intending to knock them down, but instead she will continually gaze at them, as if they are a museum exhibit. A man, on the other hand, will take out his bowling ball and seek to knock over all of her problems, much to the dismay of his wife, who is like the curator of her 'problem museum.' Even if he knocks down one pin with his bowling ball, she will remind him of the nine others that he missed, and that he has a very low bowling score. *From a man's perspective, a fair question is, "why would you set up the pins if you didn't want me to knock them down?"*

Don't try to answer that question; instead, husbands learn to love your wives by listening to them without providing solutions; especially not the wrong solutions, but even the right solution will get you nowhere. You have to learn to listen! The exclamation mark is there to announce that we men have to listen with emotions!!! These three exclamation marks, although a sign of poor English, are there to point out that I am really listening with full emotions! I apologize for being rational.

Men and women have different conversational styles. Men stay on the surface, having very goal oriented, topical conversations; women, on the other hand, tend to have deeper, more emotional conversations. A common source of fights between married couples is when the woman wants to have an emotional conversation, but the man insists on having a goal oriented conversation. A woman will often complain to a man, "you are not listening to me," but her real problem is that the man is not validating her emotions. The woman doesn't want the solution to her problem, she just wants the man to listen and show empathy toward her emotional needs. Meanwhile, the foolish man will ask, "what does her emotion have to do with anything? I wish she didn't talk so much." She Is 'talking so much' because she's fishing for words of affirmation in her husbands response.

It is hard for goal oriented men to suddenly become like their feeling oriented wives. Aren't feelings overrated? Any successful person, or professional will tell you that. By definition, being a professional means you do your job irrespective of how you feel about it. This may be true about how a doctor performs with his patients, irrespective of the fight he just had with his wife; or a pastor performs, giving guidance to his parishioners, irrespective of how he feels about his own daughter, who is an atheist. But when it comes to that doctor's relationship with his wife, or that pastor's relationship with his daughter, the principle of empathy, the force that holds all relationships together, must always take precedence over unfeeling professionalism.

This probably explains why doctors, lawyers, and especially judges, make the worst spouses--- they prefer to have goal oriented encounters, rather than emotional encounters.

For an emotional person, ***perception can become reality***; that is true, of course, before they have time to rationally figure things out. Give them the time to figure it out, don't be in a rush to correct them. They need time to walk through their emotions about some perceived reality. If you are smart you will give them time to think, instead of trying to stop them from worrying, and then you will avoid having an unnecessary argument. If you're really smart, let them come up with the solution, that way you can blame them if things go wrong.

Why does a wife need to praise her man? Why do we praise God? Why doesn't sushi swim?

Proverbs 12:25 NIV

"Anxiety weighs down the heart, but a kind word cheers it up."

If a man is carrying two bags of groceries and his wife comments how strong he is for doing so, then the man will also take his wife bag of groceries, carrying three bags himself, while his wife does not have to carry anything at all. That is how a man's ego works, but it is also how God draws us near to Him when we humbly offer up 'a sacrifice of praise.' The person doing the praising is 'sacrificing' their own ego, while drawing nearer to the person being praised.

Furthermore, praise is the opposite of evil accusation; Satan is an accuser of the brethren, and we should strive to do the opposite of what Satan does——hence, we must praise God and our spouse. The Holy Spirit 'inhabits our praises' to God, and Satan cannot live with the Spirit of God; therefore, the 'sacrifice of praise' protects our hearts from Satanic accusations.

Wives in particular must learn to speak words of edification, because men respond to praise. This is not merely because men have fragile egos, it is because praise establishes a strong relationship between the one who is praising and the one who is being praised; therefore, a wife should praise her husband the same way that the church praises Jesus. Jesus is the groom and the church is his bride, and we draw closer to Jesus when we praise him.

Married man are programmed to protect and provide for their wives. Men are like the mighty salmon: the salmon will swim upstream, against a current, dodging hungry bears, jumping over waterfalls, so that they can reach their spawning grounds and lay their eggs before they die.

Would it be appropriate to expect the salmon to perform all of these functions after having been chopped into little pieces for sushi? No, of course not, yet this is exactly what a wife does when she belittles her man for the sake of her own agenda.

My wife used to say about me, 32 years ago, when I was only 137 pounds, "I could break you in half like a stick!" Then when I got fatter, she would say, "I could roll you down the hill!"

I interjected, "hey, wait a minute! I must've been just the perfect weight at some point between 137 pounds and 237 pounds. Why didn't you say something when I was the right weight?"

She replied, "I didn't need to say anything when you were perfect."

Sushi does not swim. Here's another story about my fatness: I used to play a lot of basketball in my younger years. 32 years ago, when we were newly married, my wife used to say to me, "you have a round butt and a flat stomach." Now she says to me, "you have a flat butt and a round belly."

In response I told her, "that's because before your menopause you used to have the babies, and after menopause I am having them!"

Now that's just wrong on many levels: first of all, my wife shouldn't say derogatory things about my physical appearance----men also have feelings; secondly, men are not supposed to have babies, but if modern science could somehow make that happen, it would be a windfall for feminists. But God had a better plan than feminism.

Repeated Micromanagement (Nagging).

Men and women are equal but not the same, and viva la difference! One is the Ying, and the other is the Yang, they complete one another. Both are important, for instance, women are better micromanagers; whereas, men tend to be better macro managers. Perhaps this is due to a woman's attention to detail with regard to raising small children; meanwhile the man is out hunting large animals with his compadres. When he catches the large animal he yells out to his friends, "it's Miller time! Let's get a beer! " A woman, on the other hand, is always yelling at her children, trying to corral them to here, or to there. She is used to yelling at her kids. The problem arises when she tries to micromanage her husband as if he was one of her kids. The Bible has many scriptures about a nagging wife, this is to remind women that God is in control----not you, not your husband.

Proverbs 21:9 NIV

[9] Better to live on a corner of the roof than share a house with a quarrelsome wife.

Proverbs 27:15-16 NIV

[15] A quarrelsome wife is like the dripping of a leaky roof in a rainstorm; [16] restraining her is like restraining the wind or grasping oil with the hand.

Judges 16:16 NIV

[16] With such nagging she prodded him day after day until he was sick to death of it.

God made men with big bodies and women with big mouths, so that when the woman moves her mouth, the man moves his big body. That was just a joke, of course there are some women with big bodies. A good woman, large or small, does not nag her husband. Ladies, if he is listening, you need not talk so much, or so loud, or with so much nagging, as if you are his mother. Even God gets tired of our repetitive prayers, all the more your imperfect husband. Your husband needs you as his wife and his soulmate, not as a second mother.

Jesus turned water into wine, and I drink rum to stay married—— I call it my "wedding juice." Whenever my wife starts to nag me I drink rum and her voice starts to sound like a Jimi Hendrix guitar solo. So beautiful!

Understanding Matriarchs.

Of course there are situations when it is appropriate for a woman to lead a household. There are situations where the man is absent or dead. **Any grown man who acts like a selfish boy, should expect his wife to behave as if she is his mother----but for the rest of us men, we need respect, and we want a wife, not a second mother.** Unfortunately, modern men have a diminished role in the household, and this causes women to rise up to fill the vacuum that their men have left behind. Society perceives men as perverts and morons, this view is substantiated by the examples of Bill Clinton and Homer Simpson.

A jobless man, who fails to protect and provide for his family, loses self esteem and self respect; it gets worse if, in a bad economy, society hands him a welfare check instead of a paycheck. He gets depressed, and he becomes an easy target for his wife's nagging because he is at home instead of at a job. Subsequently, the wife does not want to stay married to a spineless, worthless, man-boy. She believes she has the right to kick him out, but what if she is a good Christian woman, and she gives him another chance?

What if, instead of kicking him out, she builds him up? What if she got behind him and invested in her man? What if when the lights went out, because he could not pay the electric bill, she made him a candle-lit dinner?

What if she believed in him because he believes in God?

What if they prayed together? What if they both invested in the lives of their children? What if she is submitted to him, as he is submitted to God, and he loved her as Christ loved the church? **A good woman is like an anchor in a stormy sea, a bad woman is like a chain and ball that will quickly take a man to the bottom of the ocean.**

What is a matriarch? The short answer: a woman who is in the unbiblical position of being the head of a family, or tribe. There are **good matriarchs,** who can function along side of her husband; and bad matriarchs, who can not tolerate a man's smallest input in her life----the **bad matriarch** is a true feminist, and she is usually divorced.

A **good matriarch** is just as rational as a man, but **she does not seek to be a man.** She sees her husband as a valuable partner in life, and shares his goals for the family. She respects her husband, and easily fights back the temptation to treat her husband as if he were one of her children. She does not micromanage him, and **she lets her man be a man.** She ages well, getting the wrinkles of laugh lines around the lips, and joy lines around the eyes, acquired from the joy of feeling God's presence, and constant squinting during praise and worship. Her years of experience and strong faith make her a beacon of light for younger women. These youngsters flock to the good matriarch for a glimpse of her compassion, wisdom, and guidance. Instead of anxiety for the future----or guilt, shame and regret for the past----the good matriarch is empowered by **her faith in God, and the power of her prayers.** The good matriarch is also described, in Proverbs 31, as a 'wife of noble character.'

In contrast to the good matriarch, the **bad matriarch** is anxious and fearful of the future. She has guilt, shame, and regret for the things that have passed. She is never content, or at peace, in the present. **She is always engaged in a power struggle with her husband, and is frequently divorced.** Instead of being a beacon of wisdom for younger women, she is jealous of their youth and beauty. She wastes all of her time and resources trying to look and feel young again, so that she can regain her youth, and become the fantasy of young men----she is a 'cougar.' She ages poorly. She hovers around the mirror, fearful of finding wrinkles or other imperfections, as if the mirror was some kind of altar to worship herself by. If she is still married, the bad matriarch will hijack her husband's authority, make a bad decision, and when things go wrong, she returns the responsibility to her man because it was always his problem to solve.

Biblically, she is wrong to covet his authority, but she is correct when she shuns responsibility, as it was never her prerogative to lead a family. It was always the man's job to be the leader, or the priest of the home; yet, a man can not lead from behind, nor can he hide behind his wife's skirt when things go wrong. The bad matriarch has put her husband in a compromised position.

Proverbs 31:10-31 NIV

[10] A wife of noble character who can find? She is worth far more than rubies. [11] Her husband has full confidence in her and lacks nothing of value. [12] She brings him good, not harm, all the days of her life. [13] She selects wool and flax and works with eager hands. [14] She is like the merchant ships, bringing her food from afar. [15] She gets up while it is still night; she provides food for her family and portions for her female servants. [16] She considers a field and buys it; out of her earnings she plants a vineyard. [17] She sets about her work vigorously; her arms are strong for her tasks. [18] She sees that her trading is profitable, and her lamp does not go out at night. [19] In her hand she holds the distaff and grasps the spindle with her fingers. [20] She opens her arms to the poor and extends her hands to the needy. [21] When it snows, she has no fear for her household; for all of them are clothed in scarlet. [22] She makes coverings for her bed; she is clothed in fine linen and purple. [23] Her husband is respected at the city gate, where he takes his seat among the elders of the land. [24] She makes linen garments and sells them, and supplies the merchants with sashes. [25] She is clothed with strength and dignity; she can laugh at the days to come. [26] She speaks with wisdom, and faithful instruction is on her tongue. [27] She watches over the affairs of her household and does not eat the bread of idleness. [28] Her children arise and call her blessed; her husband also, and he praises her: [29] "Many women do noble things, but you surpass them all." [30] Charm is deceptive, and beauty is fleeting; but a woman who fears the Lord is to be praised. [31] Honor her for all that her hands have done, and let her works bring her praise at the city gate.

What is in a family name?

The Bible never commands a married woman to 'leave her mother and father to become one flesh with her husband.' The scripture says, in Matthew 19:5, "A man shall leave his mother and father and become one flesh with his wife." A man carries his family name into his marriage. He can not go back to his mother and father's house, just as he can not run away from his family name; however, there is no such restriction on a married woman. There is a double standard here. The Bible permits a woman to 'run home to mother' if her husband fails to protect and provide for her and the kids. What gives her this right? Let us again examine the curse of Adam and Eve.

The married woman took on her husband's family name, she left her parents' home in good faith, expecting that her husband will protect and provide----**that is the curse on Adam.** God expects the man to make his marriage work, stay with his wife, and keep his family name alive. Some women have altogether circumvented the concept of a man's family name by adopting a hyphenated last name after marriage. Modern society has it done it's best to strip a man of his family name, and also of his his authority while unfairly making him retain accountability for his actions. With such a high level of responsibility and accountability attached to manhood and fatherhood, it is hard to believe that some women actually crave the authority of a man----**but that is the curse on Eve.**

We should understand that the root of all marital strife comes from the curse that God placed on Adam and Eve when they fell from the garden of Eden. Marriage comes with three rings: the engagement ring, the wedding ring, and suffer-ring. We suffer because we fight, and why do we fight? We fight to exert authority over each other, of course; but if our marriage is healthy, we will flight to restore the balance of power instead of fighting to unfairly tip the scale. In marriage you can't be selfish and you can't be lazy, and every day you have to work on improving your relationship, first with God and then with your spouse.

In any expedition, the journey is more important than the destination. I saw a bumper sticker that said, "real man ask for directions." In the journey of life we will have our shortcomings. ***A man's shortcoming is that he tries to solve problems on his own strength and wisdom, never admitting that he's lost; a woman's shortcoming is that she worries and complains too much that they are lost, even if they are not lost.*** Life is a process of coming closer to God, and closer to our spouse. It doesn't matter if we get there late, as long as we get there in good cheer, in one piece, reconciled, and not divorced.

A man has a responsibility to become one flesh with his wife. He has responsibility to carry-on his family name. He has a responsibility to raise God-fearing children. What is the woman's responsibility? Can she throw her man a bone every once in a while? Even a dog has a bone! ***Sex is not a favor, or an entitlement, it is an act of worship and a celebration of life.*** We are celebrating the exclusive relationship each of us have with God, as it is mirrored in the exclusive relationship we have with each other. We are pleasing to God through the marriage bed where we celebrate the original vows that husband and wife made on their wedding day.

Elsayed: That's good advice about sex, marriage, but what about raising children? What about raising boys to be men of God?

Chapter 7: Raising Children.

The Arrow and the Bow.

The best way to be a good mother is to first be a good wife; the best way to be a good father is to first be a good husband; and the best way to be either a good husband, or a good wife, is to first love God with all of your heart, mind, body and soul.

Success in life rarely comes from a child's triumphant independence, but rather it comes from the loving support of one's family and extended family. It takes a village to raise a child – African proverb.

The family's contribution can be in the form of setting a good example, giving loving advice, emotional backing, spiritual backing, sharing a family business, monetary backing, and setting up a support system. But most importantly a family provides a safety net that will catch the child and encourage him to stand up no matter how often he falls.

We have examined the importance of the village and the extended family in raising a child, but what is the role of the parents and the child himself? Consider this analogy: the child is like an arrow and the parent is the bow. An arrow that doesn't permit itself to be pulled back by the bow will never develop momentum, nor will it ever be trained to hit its target. Such an arrow will fall aimlessly to the ground. The bow's purpose is to train and guide the arrow, pulling back the arrow on its string, and eventually letting go. But if the bow holds onto the arrow, never letting go, this arrow also will never hit its target. Children must submit to their parents, and parents must eventually let go of their children.

The greatest danger to our children is Godlessness. We live in fast times, in a culture that is ruled by youth, skinniness, quick fixes, and government handouts instead of personal responsibility and spirituality. We can make ourselves feel good instantly with alcohol, drugs, and Internet pornography. More and more millennials are becoming atheists, because they don't want anyone, much less an invisible God, to tell them what they can or can't do. Millennials believe in self direction---"I am my own God." But, in reality, you are either accountable to God, or you are accountable to whatever you can get away with. You can easily wind up serving the kingdom of Satan instead of the kingdom of God. Godlessness leads to lawlessness, rebellion, and disrespect towards ones elders. Kids need to learn respect, gratitude, and service.

Every religion and culture teaches that we must honor and revere the elderly. In past generations the elderly were seen as the head of the family. When a matriarch or patriarch died families would crumble from a void of wisdom, love, and guidance. The most beautiful interaction is that between a grandchild, with their unending questions, and a grandparent, with their unending stories. Unfortunately, in modern times a grandparent's death is almost inconsequential. Sadly, the elderly have sunk into insignificance, and are seen as nothing more than a burden to the family. How can we turn our backs on the elderly and their time-tested wisdom? Before the written word and before computers, the elderly were the brain trust of society, and knowledge was passed through word-of-mouth alone. Now, if you don't know something, just Google it. But can a computer really teach you what life is all about? There is no substitute for time and experience, and even the wisest young person only gets wiser with age.

From boys 2 men (a famous boy band), 2 priests of the home.

The Chinese proverb says: "youth is wasted on the young."

Are you a boy with a toy, or are you a man with a plan? A boy creates more problems then he solves; a grown man solves more problems than he creates; a spiritual man is content to let someone else create and solve the problems while he purses greater spirituality, letting God solve the problems.

In a young man's life, whenever he has to choose between sex and anything else, sex always wins. Why does he always take the low road? Why didn't Adam stay single, enjoying peace, contentment, and enlightenment in the garden of Eden? Why was he willing to give it all away just to shack up with Eve and change his address to the planet earth? Two words give us the answer: "baby-baby!"

It is a man's innate need for procreation, coupled with the Biblical curse that he will have to toil for a living on earth (from his curse in Genesis, chapter 3), that dooms him to chase women, live in the 'rat race,' and always seek the perfect erectile dysfunction drug, hoping to prolong the 'baby-baby' madness way beyond what God had intended. God never intended that 90-year-old men should be making babies.

In the Bronx even old men are crazy about sex. In my clinic I've had the pleasure of telling many men, over the age of 60, that "you're too old to die fool. If you wanted to die fool you should've had this gigolo plan when you were in your 20s!" All men, except the very wisest, get into trouble because of an innate need for procreation. We commit crimes, start wars, and worse, we break our covenant with God, just for the sake of chasing a woman, or a perversion. This behavior does not necessarily change when a man ages, despite a diminished testosterone level. You would think that with less testosterone there would be more rationality, but this is not always the case. Some men never grow up.

I believe society tries to offset the ill effects of testosterone by focusing on the right of passage' from boyhood to manhood. In the Jewish culture they have bar-mitzvahs. In the African culture they have a coming of age ceremony. An African boy will live in his mother's hut until he is ready to become a man.

If the young man creates a crime or does some other testosterone fueled infraction, they don't put him in jail; instead, the male elders of the tribe will surround him and speak edifying words to build him up, telling him what he should do as a man. He is not scolded for what he has done wrong. Our society does the opposite of African culture----instead of building the young man up, we cut him down. Our nation builds more and more jails, hoping to lock up young men, only letting them out decades later, when their testosterone levels have come down to a safer level, and the men are too old to be a 'menace to society.'

Inner city men are victims of a new kind of slavery, they are living on the 'government plantation'----never given a job with a paycheck, but instead, they are stripped of their self esteem, and given a welfare check. It gets worse.

Women in the inner-city have long ago decided that they don't need a husband, saying, "I don't need a man I just want a 'baby-daddy,' The government is my only man, it gives me a welfare check, on the regular." What this is saying is that there is a new family unit that is composed of: a single mother, children, and the government. Politicians become the new man of the house, providing welfare checks, and making it easy for a woman to kick out her 'baby-daddy.'

In the old beer commercials, "Miller time," was a moment of pride that used to happen only after a man made some great, work related accomplishment; now we drink beer just to get high and forget our responsibilities because there aren't any jobs. A man gets frustrated when he cannot provide for his family, at least not as well as the government can provide through welfare checks, and then his woman kicks him out. This frustration leads a man to alcohol, drugs, crime and violence. A government who says, "stay poor we will take care of you," is a government who is fishing for votes. We don't need a Santa Claus for president who gives us gifts in exchange for votes. We need jobs. A job will enable a man to support his family, stay at home, raise the next generation, and earn respect from his wife-----and most importantly, he will be able to rise above the curse of Genesis 3:12-19.

What changes does the government need to make? We have to get rid of 'cradle to grave' entitlements and the ' nanny state.' American men have to be able to find jobs, and they should not have to complete with foreigners who are willing to work for two dollars per hour; on a broader scale, we have to tighten up trade deficits with foreign countries and bring jobs back to America. Why do we buy Chinese goods but they do not buy our goods? Broad economic change will give men a sense of pride, pride which comes from getting a pat on the back, and a boss saying, "job well done, let's have a beer." Husbands and fathers need to be appreciated by their families; young men need to be offered an education, and there needs to be jobs waiting for them when they graduate, not jails. Hard work needs to be rewarded; otherwise, we are ***incentivizing*** crime, violence, addiction, and broken homes. Capitalism, not socialism, will make more jobs. Socialism does not generate wealth, it only spends the wealth that was made through capitalism. The socialist worries about 'how the pie is cut up,' the capitalist simply 'makes more pies:' 10% of 30 pies equals 300% of one pie.

And finally, we have to reform how inner city women view marriage and government handouts. Ladies, the government is not your provider, and the politician is not your husband. Your 'baby- daddy' is your husband. Don't give up sex without a marriage commitment. Tell him, like Beyoncé says, "if you like it then you should've put a ring on it."

Both men and women have to focus on building a relationship with God first, then with the spouse, then the children, then the extended family, then the friends, then the neighborhood, then the society, then the nation, and then the world. The ripple effect of God's love will take away our pain, give us peace, and free us to live up to our full potential. After our relationship with God, which is the most important relationship, we must focus on the marriage, and the family.

Polygamy versus monogamy.

A woman takes 10 months to make a baby; a man takes 10 minutes, if that. It stands to reason that a man can procreate better, make more children, if he has multiple girlfriends and wives. And all the men from the Bronx said, "Amen!"

Why not have multiple wives and girlfriends? "If one is good, aren't two, or three, or more, better? " Is sex better after marriage? Is monogamy better? Is it 'greater later,' or, 'just get it done and move onto the next one?'

King Solomon must have been from the Bronx. When it came to women he was more interested in the quantity, not the quality of his relationships. Solomon had 700 wives and 300 girlfriends, or as the Bible calls them, concubines. What was he thinking? When was he supposed to watch football on TV? I don't think he was very bright, someone probably told him that a concubine was the combination of a conch, a cucumber, and a porcupine – – – he got interested and had enough money to buy 300 concubines, not knowing that these were women.

In 2 Chronicles, chapter 1, Salomon asks God for wisdom and knowledge, but he didn't ask for a heart that guides him about marriage. Tragically, Salomon forgot the true joy comes from a heart that seeks God first, and then a monogamous relationship with only one woman, thereafter. Solomon was miserable because he believed that 1000 imperfect wives and girlfriends could love him perfectly, as only God can.

King Solomon secretly craved monogamous love; hence, he authored the song of Solomon, also known as "the song of songs." This piece, which reads like a love novel, was a tribute to the love between one man and one woman. Despite his wisdom, his knowledge, his power, his wealth, his rationality, Solomon's relationships with women were all superficial. Despite having so many women in his life, Solomon never himself experienced deep love between himself and one woman.

God made sex pleasurable so that we would procreate, but sex between a husband and wife is so much more than just procreation. Every time a married couple has sex they are celebrating oneness before God: oneness with each other, and oneness with God, individually. Sex, in the purest sense, is a way to worship God; it is not a favor, or an entitlement between human beings. A strong marriage begins with two individuals first seek intimacy with God, and then they seek intimacy with one another. Why seek a monogamous relationship? Because God is big on exclusivity. Just as God wants us to seek Him above all other relationships, God designed marriage as a mirror of the exclusive bond that we have with God.

The song of Solomon is full of envy that Solomon had against those who have found deep love in a monogamous relationship. King Solomon would have traded all 700 wives and 300 concubines just for one good porcupine. That is not a joke, having a spouse is like hugging a porcupine. Love hurts, but it's worth the trouble because in the end the sex is better; it really is 'greater later,' but the later takes a long time, perhaps a lifetime to achieve. At times love will cause you sleepless nights, and rob you of your peace, but it is still worth it. We are to grow old together, growing closer to each other, and closer to God every day.

Marriage is the attempt to love only one imperfect person, unconditionally. We are to stay together for life and raise children of good character. Bacteria proliferate in minutes, humans raise children over a lifetime. God judges a man by the quality of his progeny, not the quantity. Men are called by God to be priests in their homes. Joshua 24:15, "as for me and my house we will serve the Lord."

If you want to know about a man, just look at the character of his wife and children.

When a man dies and stands before God, he will be asked by God about the actions of his wife and children, not just his own actions.

When my wife and I first met and things started to get serious, she asked me if she was going to be the first of many Muslim wives. I told her that one wife was like a single hole in the head, and that if I had a second and third wife, my brains would leak out faster and faster; therefore, I intended to be monogamous for life.

Erection versus Enlightenment.

Testosterone causes a young man to think of sex every nine seconds. After the age of 35 all men lose their youthful level of testosterone; the highest level is when a man is 19 years of age; and over the age of 50, over 50% of men have a low testosterone level. As a mature man, age 58, I benefit from a shrinking level of testosterone. For the sake of my sanity I refuse to take testosterone replacement therapy. I have come to the conclusion that I will never allow testosterone to rob me of my peace.

A young man is like a wide mouth bass, happily swimming in the lake, until he encounters the hook of a woman. A young woman will spend her entire life sharpening that hook. If she's even more cunning she'll put a Barb on that hook to prevent him from slipping off, that's why they call a girl's favorite doll, 'Barbie'. She then hides the hook with his favorite meal and drowns his senses in a sea of his favorite alcoholic beverage. Once the lure is in the water, she makes it giggle and wiggle, until the poor, hapless man succumbs to temptation.

Why is it that a young man, who takes one look at a pretty girl, is so quick to forget about his male friends, and surrender his peace? It is almost a reflexive action. If the girl is pretty enough he will fight other men in order to win her attention, just like moose in the rutting season. Pretty girls can afford to be crazy because there will always be guys lining up just to get a chance with them. This reminds me of an old Abbott and Costello movie. At the end of the movie, when the police are dragging away Costello's gorgeous yet evil wife to jail, Costello turns to Abbot and says, "hey Abbott, the next time I get married I'm going to marry an ugly woman. That's because if she's ugly she'll never leave me, and if she leaves me who cares – – – she was ugly! "

We have a hard life here on earth. Raising a family is a really hard chore. Yet God did not call us to be celibate monks living in a monastery; instead, we are to live in this world, procreate in the world, and yet not be of it. We have to have ambition in order to succeed. We also need cash.

The perception of money changes with time and it is related to our pursuit of procreation. Someone once said, "when you're young and alone, $50 is a lot of money in your pocket; when you've got a girlfriend, $100 is a lot of money in your pocket; when you're married, $500 is a lot of money in your pocket; when you've got a house and kids, $1000 is a lot of money in your pocket."

There's a lot more to life than just money, but it's hard to be a minimalist, a maximalist, or a rebel when you have a hole in your pocket. And if you are a guy, you should ask, "who put that hole there?" In the biblical story of 'Adam and Eve,' it was Eve who put that hole in Adam's pocket. All Eve had to do was giggle and wiggle, and then it seemed like a pretty good idea for Adam to eat of the forbidden fruit. After Eve enticed Adam to take a bite, God put a curse on Adam, forcing him to toil for a living for the rest of his life, Genesis 3:16–17. Now he has to work for a living, instead of having everything given for free in the garden of Eden. A man's life is hard. He becomes a beast of burden for his family. There is no peace. Men usually die first, before our spouses, because this is the only way that he can 'rest in peace.'

Here is the story that shows just how early in a boy's life he becomes a beast of burden. It's a story about two innocent eight-year-old kids, named Johnny and Sally.

Johnny and Sally.

Johnny and Sally were playing in the meadow, when Johnny challenged Sally to a race. "Let's race to that Oak tree." Before Sally could agree, Johnny had already bolted off towards the tree. When he arrived there first he started gloating over Sally, "you're so slow, I could easily beat you in a race! "

Johnny was feeling charitable so he offered to race Sally to the top of the tree and then back down to the ground. Before Sally could agree, Johnny was already halfway up the tree, and by the time she had reached only the second branch, Johnny had already climbed to the top and was on his way down.

Once on the ground, Johnny again started to gloat over his victory. Sally was annoyed, but she noticed that while Johnny was gloating he had his eyes fixed on her undergarments. This was possible because Sally was on the third branch of the tree.

Suddenly, Sally remembered the lesson that her mother had taught her. She looked down on Johnny was still gloating and asked him, "are you looking at my panties?"

Johnny was taken aback by her candor, but strangely he replied with the truth, "why, yes." He didn't want to keep it a secret anymore that he was fascinated by Sally's undergarments. Maybe this was his chance to see more!

Sally smirked at him, and then went on to explain, "my momma says that these panties will one day control your life, Johnny. These panties will make you climb up the tree, and down the tree, run across the field, and back again. Over and over again. All for these panties! "

Right away, Johnny's eyes grew big, and he stopped gloating. Somehow he knew that his life was about to get a whole lot more complicated.

It is a good thing that marriage happens when we are young and foolish, like a thief in the night, because otherwise, no one in his or her right mind would get married, not if we were to give it even a minute of thought. It is harder to get married late in life because both men and women become more selective, to the point where no one is good enough for them to marry. This is because their eyes are wide open, and they are not willing to let anyone rob them of their peace. But let's face it, without the lure of sex, it is unlikely that anyone would get married.

Why is a young man so quick to surrender his peace? Perhaps it is because of a young man's lack of experience, or perhaps he had a bout of 'gonadal thinking'----that is, thinking with the wrong head. Let's talk about a young man's lack of experience, because there's absolutely nothing that can be done to save a man from 'gonadal thinking'. A young man is highly opinionated, yet he lacks knowledge and experience; in contrast, an old man has less opinion, more knowledge, and plenty of experience.

If you harvest wine too quickly it is still grape juice; but if you wait for years to pass, the grape juice turns into the finest wine. Right now, I'm at the youth of old age, and I feel as if a veil has been lifted from my eyes; but don't worry, men and young men, you'll get your chance to grow old, and soon enough you will have your day of clarity. **Enlightenment is more valuable, and yet it is far less costly, than erections.**

Just remember, behind every great man is a great woman; and behind every fallen man is yet another woman. A man can carry on with only one hole in the head, and a great woman may be required to keep him humble and well grounded. But a mistress soon takes on the status of a second wife, she adds another hole to the man's head, and makes his life infinitely more complicated. The man' brains leak out twice as fast, and he is stricken down from his previous greatness. Hell hath no fury as a woman scorned.

Ambition versus contentment.

My favorite advice to young people is to find someone who has already been through what you're going through, preferably 10 or 12 years older than you, and seek an ongoing mentorship with them. Fifty percent of acquiring wisdom is knowing what you don't know, the other fifty percent is to seek mentorship with someone who already knows.

Parents are the original mentors in a child's life. The fifth commandment of the Bible says that we must honor our parents if we are to live a long and prosperous life; disrespecting our parents predisposes us to an unsuccessful life and an early death (spiritual death, if not physical death).

There are very few self-made millionaires. Most wealthy people either inherited wealth from their parents, or grew it by adapting lessons from their parents (The book titled, 'Rich dad Poor dad,' comes to mind). You are better off learning from your parent's mistakes, rather than making those same mistakes on your own. History has a way of repeating itself, the apple doesn't fall far from the tree, and genetics don't lie..

Why did my parents love me even when I was a rude, young, highly opinionated man-child-with- pimples? The following is a poem, *ode to a young man,* 'for all of those parents who have a rebellious son. Just hang on, you see I didn't turn out too badly----but it took fifty-five years for me to grow up.

The saying goes, "employ a teenager before they find out that they don't know everything." All of that bravado must be worth something----shouldn't it? It is good for a young man to be goal oriented and ambitious, and it is good for an old man to look back at his life and find peace and contentment.

To find peace in life we have to learn how to temper our ambition with a sense of contentment. A child can be content just to play in an empty cardboard box. As the child grows it is good that he has ambition to make something of himself. After many decades of a career, a family, a house, and other possessions, it is once again important for man to learn how to be content without many of these things. It is important for a man to learn how to say, "enough is enough," and turn his ambitious pursuits inwards, toward finding peace, contentment, and enlightenment.

My priorities changed when my granddaughter was born. Now, instead of taking friends and business associates out, I'm content to sit on my deck at home, cook on my grill, and play with my granddaughter. Another relatively inexpensive activity, that brings me great joy, is to go on road trips with my granddaughters family. We bring my son and his wife along because sometimes the baby needs to be fed, changed, and put to sleep.

When we are old, the forces of natural aging catch up with us, to the point where contentment is as simple as it was when we were children. This time we are content merely to have normal bodily functions, when we can see and pee, and have a normal bowel movement. We forget names but we remember faces, particularly the faces of those we love the most. Old-age has facetiously been called a 'second childhood,' but I look at it as an opportunity to go back to finding peace. Only this time, instead of playing in a cardboard box, you are in a pine box, six feet under the ground, and you finally find peace.

Early in our life it is good to have ambition, to make a name for ourselves, to plant a seed. Later in our life it is good to be content with what we have, prune back the excess in our life, and learn to make do with less. A mature man knows when to downsize, so as to focus on what is really important in life. In the end, you can't take your toys with you when you die. The wisest old people focus their efforts entirely on ways to get closer to God. Nothing else matters towards the end of life.

When a boy or a grown man first knows the Lord he says, "Lord, I will live all of my days for you." When an old man knows the Lord, he says, "Lord even if I had only one day left on earth, I would live it all for you." The old man's one day is more precious than a young man's decade, or a grown man's year.

The sweetest surrender comes from a mature heart, one that has, time and time again, chosen to believe. The old man has the greatest depth of love for God, because his love is the summation of decades of history. The summation of failures and triumphs that have led him to this great love of God, in this precious moment.

Ode to a Young Man.

Just because you have a beard It doesn't mean you have wisdom.

Just because you have an opinion it doesn't mean you have knowledge.

Just because you are a male it doesn't mean that you have grown to be a man.

Just because you have muscles it doesn't make you a man of honor.

Just because your mother cleans your room and does your laundry it doesn't mean that you understand women.

Where can I begin to teach you? Are you a man with a plan, or merely a boy with a toy? For starters, you have to learn to follow before you can lead.

You can start to understand women by first respecting your mother.

Learn to be a man of honor by following the fifth commandment of the Bible: honor and respect your parents.

Elsayed: what is your advice about raising girls to be God-fearing women?

Abdullah: I'll take a pass on that one! I've got no clue. First you have the PMS, then you have the menopause, and then finally a woman becomes as rational as a man. That's about the extent of my knowledge of women.

Elsayed: Oh no! My great counselor is stumped for words! All right, I'll ask you about an easier topic. What about growing old gracefully after you've already raised your family?

Abdullah: I can handle that one. Here are some essays about grace throughout old age.

Chapter 8: Growing Old Gracefully.

Trouble.

Proverbs 23:3, the prudent man sees trouble and takes refuge but the naïve continue on.

The wise man foresees trouble and hides himself. He doesn't go looking for trouble. If trouble finds him he doesn't try to beat trouble down; trouble cannot be averted, nor can peace be restored, by fighting. Instead, the wise man hides himself from trouble, and he makes preparations to avoid the ill consequences of trouble. Things happen to you either out of design or out of default. It's always a good idea to have a plan and make good choices.

What kind of preparations does the wise man make? Here are a few examples: if you want to avoid the trouble of poverty, get an education and find yourself a job; if you want to avoid the trouble of loneliness, learn how to respect women, starting with your mother, comb your hair, and then maybe you'll get a girlfriend; if you get married and want to avoid the trouble of a quarrel, learn that it is more important to be happy and unselfish than it is to be right. Most divorces involve highly opinionated people who are not content to wait for hell, they strive to create hell on earth. These kind of people are real magnets for trouble.

As we mature there is a natural progression from opinion to experience, from experience to knowledge, from knowledge to wisdom, and finally from wisdom to spirituality. The older I get, the more I try to curtail my opinion. Opinions are nothing more than a collection of thoughts that are seen through the filter of ones own personal bias. Experience is a great teacher, but it is better to learn from other people's mistakes. Knowledge is a compilation of experiences, both personal and collective, but knowledge can only take you so far. Wisdom is the ability to apply knowledge to every particular circumstance. Spirituality is when God intervenes and gives us answers to questions that we didn't even have the wisdom to ask. Jeremiah 3:33, the Lord says "cry out onto me and I will teach you many great and unsearchable things."

I try to know more than I can say. I try to rely on God's wisdom rather than my own. I try not to be seduced by the world. I choose to be humbled by the presence of God. The lights of the world grow strangely dim as the glory of God shines more brightly in my life.

God's wisdom applied to my life strengthens my faith and gives me a testimony. My testimony, and the blood of Jesus, and the word of God, are the best weapons to fight off Satan during this life, according to the book of Revelation.

The older I get, the more I appreciate and respect my parents. Now that I'm sixty years old, I am less likely to take the advice of anyone under the age of thirty-five. My parents were the first to teach me how to listen. They taught me that there is a reason why we have two ears and one mouth: we are to listen twice as much as we speak. When we are young, fueled by hormones, we tend to have an opinion about many things but knowledge about nothing. The same kid, who is last to listen to a parent's advise, will be the first one to ask for help when he suffers the consequence of not following that same advice. That is why in every culture and civilization the young are expected to respect their parents and anyone who is older than them. It behooves us to learn from the older generation.

My father wrote an essay titled, "I am expanding even as I shrink." It is an essay about the aging process, and how although our world shrinks as we age, our wisdom and our spirituality expands. My father writes about downsizing one's life as we get older: making less money, going to fewer parties; becoming more selective in what we read, eat, and with whom we socialize. When we get older we pick our battles very carefully, avoiding them almost entirely.

We go with the flow. Old people don't have time for trouble. Our vision gets weaker so that we don't see other people's flaws, our hearing gets poor so that we don't hear every argument that someone accosts us with. The wisest old people focus their efforts entirely on ways to get closer to God. Nothing else matters in the end of life.

Grandpa Loves to Putter.

Fathers are the perfection of manhood, and grandfathers are the perfection of fatherhood. A grandpa is someone who has successfully raised his own children to the point where these children have had children of their own. Good or bad, grandchildren come with little victories and little problems of their own. Little kids little problems, big kids big problems. But before these problems become huge, a grandchild, age 10 or less, provides a grandpa an easy and productive opportunity to putter around the house and share his wisdom.

Deuteronomy 11:19 NIV
[19] Teach your children, talking with them when you sit at home and when you walk along the road, when you lie down and when you get up.

Grandchildren need grandparents and grandparents need grandchildren——It is a match made in heaven. When I was a small child, I used to think that God looked like my grandfather. That was because I had such high reverence for both God and my grandfather, I naively thought that they looked alike. I am 60 years old now, and I had my first son born to me when I was 25 years old, and his name is Adam. Adam got married to Lindsey and now we have three beautiful granddaughters as a result. My daughter, Tara, married a pastor named JP, and as a result we have two more beautiful granddaughters and a grandson. The total: five granddaughters, one grandson. My other son, Raza, is carefree: no wife, no children.

I told Lindsey, my daughter in law, that I love to putter around the house. She said," no, you are not a putter, you are a 'domestic engineer.'" Lindsey was trying to give me a more glamorous title by calling me an "engineer," rather than just a humble, puttering grandfather. Such a puttering grandfather is one who pays attention to detail, he sees what needs to be done, and takes care of everyone else's needs before his own. I prefer to be called a puttering grandfather. To whom much is granted, much will be expected; If a grandfather takes care of the little things, then the big things will fall into place by the grace of God. A grandfather is a catalyst to bring spirituality to all of the generations that came after him.

In the game of golf sometimes you drive the long ball, sometimes you putt the short ball, but both are important, as you cannot always hit a hole-in-one with a long ball. Skill at hitting the long ball is complemented by skill at hitting the short ball. Puttering is important to golf. What is the dictionary definition of the word: Putter? putter: to occupy oneself in a desultory but pleasant manner, doing a number of small tasks or not concentrating on any thing in particular: early morning is the best time of the day to putter around the garden.

Funny, the dictionary talks about 'puttering around the garden.' If Adam and Eve were more proficient in puttering around the garden of Eden, then maybe they would have ignored the serpent who lured them into eating the fruit from the tree of knowledge. Too much knowledge is dangerous. It is better to humbly putter with the little knowledge you have. As you walk with the Lord, going along puttering, ask the Lord to give you wisdom. God will tell you what you need to know, and when you need to know it; wisdom will come in God's time and portion, not too soon, not too much, as what might get you into trouble, especially if you start to think that you are your own god. The most ambitious human activity is a waste of time if it does not advance the kingdom of God.

Genesis 2:15-17 NIV

[15] The Lord God took the man and put him in the Garden of Eden to work it and take care of it. [16] And the Lord God commanded the man, "You are free to eat from any tree in the garden; [17] but you must not eat from the tree of the knowledge of good and evil, for when you eat from it you will certainly die."

In Jeremiah 33:3, God promises us that if we cry out to him for wisdom, then he will answer questions that we did not even have the wisdom to ask. The right questions come to us when we are in step with God, while we putter around in the garden of life. Sometimes we try to put God in a box. "If I pray like this, then God will answer my prayers like that." God already knows what is in our hearts, and in our minds, and in our prayers. God created prayer so that we could talk to Him, as we go on a lifelong journey with Him. He does not need our advise, or for us to tell Him what we need. God honors our relationship throughout our walk with Him. Our faith matures with time and through hard lessons from life. The only reason God wants to hear your prayers is because He loves you, as He walks with you for all of your days. ***God cannot be manipulated, but he can be loved!*** He wants to hear your voice because he cherishes having a relationship with you.

Jeremiah 33:3 NIV

[3] 'Call to me and I will answer you and tell you great and unsearchable things you do not know.'

God is interested in our availability, not our ability. God does not call the equipped, but He equips those He calls. We must walk with Him as we putter around this earth. Although we have our own talents, all we really bring to the table is our faith, our obedience, and our humility. Before the fall from the garden of Eden, Adam and Eve would take long, wonderful walks with God in the coolness of the morning, and their relationship with the Lord was perfect. But people never leave well enough alone, as we are not content to just walk with God. We forget that our hearts are a temple for the Holy Spirit——the heart is the house of the Lord.

Haggai 1:7-9 NIV

[7] This is what the Lord Almighty says: "Give careful thought to your ways. [8] Go up into the mountains and bring down timber and build my house, so that I may take pleasure in it and be honored, " says the Lord. [9] "You expected much, but see, it turned out to be little. What you brought home, I blew away. Why?" declares the Lord Almighty. "Because of my house, which remains a ruin, while each of you is busy with your own house.

It is better to walk slowly with the Lord, than it is to run faster than your angels can fly. By the time your angels catch up with you, you will be in a twisted heap of trouble——such is the outcome of an unguided life, or worse, a life that is guided by Satan. The saying goes, "someone who doesn't take loving advice will have Satan as a guide." Adam and Eve should have been content to take care of the little things in the garden of Eden, instead of chasing after worldly knowledge and power that they sought by eating the forbidden fruit.

The devil told Eve that she could know everything that God knows and become like God herself. And then that stupid, non-puttering, lazy Adam, who was not a grandfather as yet, stood around and let his wife talk to the devil. He should have chased the serpent away, and slapped that fruit out of Eve's hands, but maybe he just wanted to appease Eve because she wiggled and giggled.

Adam actually blamed God for the "defective woman" God gave him, but Adam had no defense after he ate the fruit from Eve's hand. Adam would be cursed to toil on the earth forever, all the while being nagged by Eve. Eve's curse brought painful childbirth, and she craved for Adam's authority and dominion, but she wanted none of his accountability: Eve wanted to be the man, but Adam had to be the man. Adam and Eve had died, spiritually.

The devil is in the details. The devil will have you leave a banana peel on the floor and he will tell you that it won't be a problem until someone slips on it, and it still won't be a problem until someone has one foot in the grave and the other foot on the banana peel. Finally, when he has you right where he wants you, the devil will taunt you, saying, "Hah, looks like you have a problem!" He will say this while he's shoveling dirt over your grave, burying you and your laziness, all because of you lacked foresight, and you did not pay attention to detail. You took your eye off the eternal prize, which is the kingdom of God. You should have been puttering.

Grandpas and grandmas are the shield bearers for the next generation. A shield bearer, in ancient Roman times, was someone who protected and assisted the soldier by carrying weapons and by erecting a shield to protect him from the enemy's incoming fiery darts.

Similarly, grandparents are to protect and assist younger generations who lack experience, and are often distracted by the bread and butter issues of raising children. Children are sponges for love and guidance, and they have so many questions that a grandpa can answer. Children need to be loved and read to. It takes a village to raise God-fearing children——that includes parents, grandparents, aunts, and uncles. The government cannot raise your child.

Joshua 24:15 NIV

[15] But if serving the Lord seems undesirable to you, then choose for yourselves this day whom you will serve. But as for me and my household, we will serve the Lord.

Deuteronomy 5:9-10 NIV

[9] You shall not bow down to them [idols] or worship them; for I, the Lord your God, am a jealous God, punishing the children for the sin of the parents to the third and fourth generation of those who hate me, [10] but showing love to a thousand generations of those who love me and keep my commandments.

The greatest mission is to raise good children and grandchildren, but you cannot teach what you do not know. If your mission only serves you, and not your family, and not your God, don't be surprised if your mission fails; on the other hand, God will grant you success if your put serving the kingdom of God as your primary goal, and raising your family a secondary goal.

Matthew 6:33-34 NIV

[33] But seek first his kingdom and his righteousness, and all these things will be given to you as well. [34] Therefore do not worry about tomorrow, for tomorrow will worry about itself. Each day has enough trouble of its own.

God owns the mansion on the hill, and you only own the tiny sandcastle on the beach. Without God, you are the king of a very small kingdom, a kingdom of one, and your sandcastle will be washed away with the next incoming tide. God, on the other hand, is the purveyor of the eternal kingdom of heaven. If you honor God's kingdom, then not only will He grant you eternal life, but He will also honor your little temporary kingdom on earth. If you become a sweeper in the mansion that belongs to God, then God will adopt you as a child of His. God will come, like the good father, who brings a plastic shovel and pail to the beach, where his child is building a sandcastle. God honors what is important to you if you honor what is important to Him, and He will help you in your insignificant kingdom, as long as you seek first the kingdom of God and take part in His higher calling. You find God's purpose for your life when you seek first His kingdom.

Psalm 84:10 NIV

[10] Better is one day in your courts than a thousand elsewhere; I would rather be a doorkeeper in the house of my God than dwell in the tents of the wicked.

Puttering is like a prayer that you do while your hands and feet are moving. Prayer doesn't prepare us for great work, it is the great work––when we work, we use short arms and short legs, but when pray it is God who works, and His arms are longer than ours, and His feet are bigger. God assigns angels to go out ahead of us to prepare the way and lighten the load of our journey. Puttering directs our angels to know in which direction we want them to move, and what things and people are important to us.

Angels cultivate our circumstances so that we can accomplish great and mighty things to advance the kingdom of God, a kingdom that only God's children can advance on earth, and in heaven.

In summary: do what little you can, pray, and God will do the rest. An idle mind is the devil's workshop. It is better to putter around in the garden of life, while constantly seeking the Lord.

Generations

For each generation raising children comes with new challenges and new solutions. Raising children requires that you use distractions: the current generation uses the iPad, my generation used videos, grandma's generation used television and before that, great grandma used stone tablets. The only thing written on those stone tablets were the Ten Commandments. How boring. Great grandma would get angry at her children when they wouldn't pay attention to the reading of the stone tablets, particularly the part about the fifth commandment: "thou shall honor thy parents.... " If they still wouldn't listen she would throw those stone tablets at her kids to get their attention.

Providing discipline for great grandma's children was much easier than it is today. She would simply resort to the biblical scripture, "spare the rod and spoil the child. " Corporal punishment was permissible back then; it is not permissible today, if you hit a child today you have a CPS case set against you. Young people don't even want to hear advice from their elders, not if the same information can be googled without any emotional risk.

It is so common to hear young parents say, "I'm going to raise my children different from the way my parents raised me! I won't even let my mother see her grandchildren. Not ever." Does that sound familiar? History has a way of repeating itself. Choices we make now will affect the generations to come. Where will your family be in thirty years? After your parents are dead and gone, and you will be middle aged, and your kids will be disrespecting you. Thirty years go by in the blink of an eye.

Showing love to the older generation requires taking a risk. Love is risky, but just as the surgeon's knife causes bleeding, no one complains after the cancer is cut out and the patient is healed. God's word is the surgeons knife. God's love is our life blood. God's son, Jesus, is the master surgeon. During surgery you bleed a little, but not enough to kill you, and then God replenishes your love and revives your heart. You wake up from surgery, and you are cured.

One generation ago your mother gave birth to you, and a generation before that your mother was born to your grandmother, and so on. One thing that all mothers have in common is anxiety. Mothers are worriers and fathers are warriors. A good Christian should not go through life suffering in "the cycle of fear; " instead, we should live a victorious life in "the cycle of hope." All mothers battle anxiety. Mothers are anxious about all of life's variables that they cannot control. She loses control when others don't subscribe to her fearful world view. Loss of control leads to anger, especially anger at those who don't let her control them. Ultimately anger leads to a loss of faith, which leads to more anxiety, and the 'cycle of fear' perpetuates itself, over and over again.

To all of you young mothers, if you are not anxious about your infant yet, just wait 13 or 15 years when your baby becomes a teenager. For those of you with daughters, let's hope that your daughter doesn't develop PMS at the same time that you develop menopause, as would be the case if you were approximately thirty years old when your daughter was born.

History repeats itself in both the individual and in the generation. Some of this generational repetition is good – – – it is our culture, our creed, our pride, what I call our ***generational wisdom***; but there is also a dark side, or what I call our ***generational curse***. The sins of the father will be visited upon the son, for generations and generations. We are all still paying for the original sin of Adam and Eve after they were kicked out of the garden of Eden. Whether it is the ancient sin of Adam and Eve, or merely a lapse in proper child rearing, these sins all add up and create an errant life process for generations to come. In order to break the generational curse we cannot rely on human wisdom or human strength; instead, we must rely solely on God: the love of God, the word of God, and the sacrificial blood of Jesus.

The Bronx is rich in stories of incredible courage, persistence, love, and reconciliation. Against all odds this seventeen year old girl, daughter of one of my heroin addicted patients, proved that the generational curse could be reversed and a family could be reconciled. My patient, Felix, was alone and suicidal, before he received this timely text message from his daughter. He had two failed marriages, with several children from each x-wife, he was tired and depressed, not knowing if he could hold on to life until tomorrow. He was suicidal. But God sent him an angel----his own daughter. Somehow she got the courage to go against what everyone had said about her father, and without the fear of rejection, she showed him the unconditional love of Jesus in a text message. Here is the actual text:

"But I want you in my life no matter what anyone says. I'm not gonna be that kid who hates their father their whole life and when they pass I feel guilty. I want to have that bond and for me it's never too late. I mean you screw up so many times but yet I still keep coming back. That should tell you something about me. I want a father and daughter relationship with you ... Yea you scared me for life but it's never to late for me to forgive you. 😊 Maybe spending the day with me can actually cheer you up."

After Felix received this text he got the strength to go on living. Father and daughter were reconciled. They spent the whole next day together, and healing started to take place in both of their hearts. Felix could not hold back the tears, bawling loudly, unable to read when he first shared his daughter's text with me. I grabbed his cell phone wanting to quickly read the text that saved his life. But when I started reading it for myself, I too began crying with buckets of tears. Such a beautiful letter! This letter was obviously inspired by God. It was love in action. It was every bit as eloquent as the Bible's chapter on love in 1Corinthians, chapter 13.

But it gets better. One month after he shared his daughter's text with me, he came back to my clinic five days ago, and I was expecting to hear some little praise report from him. I thought it was enough of a praise report that he was still alive, and not a victim of suicide, or a heroin overdose, but I could never be prepared for all that he had to tell me.

After reconciling with his daughter, Felix went to a Pentecostal church and dedicated his life to Jesus. He then armed himself with injectable vials of narcan, which is an antidote for heroin overdose. He made his rounds in the mean streets of the Bronx, starting his self imposed shift at twelve midnight. Within a two week period he saved the lives of five overdosed heroin addicts, on behalf of Jesus, the Master Physician who he now follows.

But it gets better. God gifted him with the power of healing. The healing started with his own neck pain and stiffness which, as his doctor I can tell you was originally from multiple herniated cervical discs, the result of two car accidents. He told me that his neck got healed the moment he got saved by Jesus, and then he swiveled his neck around in every direction, just to prove to me that he was miraculously healed, despite being off pain medication.

But it gets better. Felix has been stopping random people in the street, people who were walking with crutches, canes, and rollator walkers, asking them, "Do you have a strong faith in Jesus?" If they said, "yes," he would proceed to heal them, and they would put away their crutches, canes, and rollator walkers and move on, unassisted. And so began the street evangelism of my patient, Felix, who was once a worrier but is now a warrior for the Lord.

Luke 9:1-6 NIV

[1] When Jesus had called the Twelve together, he gave them power and authority to drive out all demons and to cure diseases, [2] and he sent them out to proclaim the kingdom of God and to heal the sick. [3] He told them: "Take nothing for the journey---no staff, no bag, no bread, no money, no extra shirt. [4] Whatever house you enter, stay there until you leave that town. [5] If people do not welcome you, leave their town and shake the dust off your feet as a testimony against them." [6] So they set out and went from village to village, proclaiming the good news and healing people everywhere.

But it gets better. It turns out that Felix is a famous rapper, and HBO is doing a documentary about him. Maybe my book will get a shout out on HBO! All of this has happened within the past month, ever since Felix and I prayed together, and his daughter showed him the unnatural, unconditional love of Jesus. Satan wanted him 'six feet under,' but Jesus healed him and proceeded to exalt him to a level higher than the angles! To God be the glory!

John 20:21 NIV

[21] Again Jesus said, "Peace be with you! As the Father has sent me, I am sending you."

Elsayed: Your father and I share a name, he is "SYED," and I am, "ELSAYED." Tell me more about your father.

Abdullah: my father is 94 years old and he lives in one of my sister's house. He is a very humble man, despite being a doctor, a researcher, and a writer himself. Before his first birthday he became an orphan, as his father died of leukemia. The following story is about his meekness and how it helped him befriend a bully when he was just a boy growing up in India.

My Friend, The Bully: How My Meek Father Inherited The World.

Matthew 5:5 NIV

[5] Blessed are the meek, for they will inherit the earth.

Luke 6:27 NIV

[27] "But to you who are listening I say: Love your enemies, do good to those who hate you,

I often questioned how meekness can be a blessing. Jesus said, "the meek shall inherit the earth." Perhaps that scripture explains how I became a great grandfather last year, despite myself being a fatherless child who grew up poor in India. Born in 1928, my father died of leukemia before my first birthday. Even before the age of ten I would fantasize, not only that I had a father, but I also had fantasies about myself becoming a father – – – the kind of perfect father that every child wishes they had. Many decades later, and by God's grace, I am a great grandfather. I must say that I "inherited the whole world" when I first held my great granddaughter in my arms. This is the story of how a meek little boy, growing up fatherless in India, has "inherited the world," and has survived in that cruel world.

I was an easy target for the school bully, Mohamed Ali. That was his real name. He was born long before the boxer, and yet both of them could 'float like a butterfly and sting like a bee.' We were both only seven or eight years of age, but I had the physique of a thinker and he had the physique of a thumper. He knew that I would neither fight, nor run, nor scream for help. He often challenged me to a fist fight, or a wrestling match, at the end of the school day. To make matters worse he would present this challenge at the start of the day. I would be petrified at the prospect all through the school hours, praying that by some miracle my father would appear at the school gate to rescue me from this rogue.

During my beatings, my mind would be gradually transported to another place. A fantasy place where there was no pain. A place where I imagined that my father was running toward me, freeing me from the beating, and chasing the bully away. I could once again feel the pain when I was snapped back into reality, but the thing that hurt the most had nothing to do with physical pain.

The greatest pain was being separated from the love of my father, and knowing that my father was not coming to rescue me. Not now, not ever. Where was my father, in heaven? What good was he doing for me up there in heaven? My prayer went unanswered; my father had died when I was eleven months old.

By the age of two, I had already lost a baby's natural fear of strangers. I would go to a stranger if they would extend a loving hug toward me. My mother was afraid that I would run off with any stranger who would show me the slightest bit of affection. I was a very sensitive child and, even before I could talk, I have memories in which I was acutely aware that my father was gone. In particular, I would look at all men and think, "maybe he is my father."

Back in those days even poor people had servants. I had a servant – caretaker, his name was Husan Khan. When I was just a toddler Mr Khan would take me out on the town. One of his favorite places to take me was to his friend, the dried fruits vendor. Mr. Khan must have told the dried fruit vendor that I was an orphan; meanwhile, I must of been sizing up the vendor as one of my possible 'dad candidates'.

From the first day that vendor found out that I was an orphan he showed me incredible love and compassion. He would take me up in his arms, hug me, hold me, kiss me, and feed me little pieces of dried fruit. Every time we would visit him this man would cry streams of tears for me.

He was deeply worried about my dark, fatherless, future. To this day, I'm 90 years old, and I still love to eat dried fruits and nuts----my long life can be explained by diet rich in almonds, walnuts, cashews and peanuts. These are my comfort foods, and it's easy to know why. It was the love that my substitute father, the dried fruit and nut vender, had shown me at a time when I was seeking love.

On other occasions, Mr. Khan would take me through some of the seedier parts of town. On one street corner there was this young woman, she smelled really good and she had a liking towards me. Mr. Khan had told her that I was an orphan. That was all she needed to hear.

She immediately took me up in her arms and cried for me. Later in life I found out that she had been pregnant and had recently given birth to a stillborn baby. I don't know what she saw in me, perhaps I provided some kind of connection to her dead child.

All I knew is that she smelled like roses and she was always dressed in the brightest colors. Strangely, I remembered her name, it was Shanti, the Hindi word for 'peace.' I remembered her name because some rude person would constantly shout it out. He would shout out, over and over again. Later in life I learned that Shanti was a prostitute.

For all of these people, the bully, the dried fruit vendor, and the prostitute, God used my meekness, my innocence, my weakness, as a source for bringing out the good in all of them. I became an opportunity for others to disconnect with their reality and to find a moment of peace within my reality. God also blessed me with a moment of peace. My 'disconnect moment' was furbished by my quest to find my earthly father, whether in dreams or in visions, but never in reality. I'm ninety years old and I'm still on a quest to find my father in heaven, my God. As long as I seek God, I will always be a comfort for those who are in pain.

Giving others comfort has become the basis for my studying medicine and later psychiatry. My son, who is also a medical doctor, is the son of a psychiatrist. That makes my son either perfectly sane or perfectly insane!

But let's get back to my friend, the bully. Mysteriously, after the first brutal beating, I was spared another beating. The bully seemed content with some rough-housing before letting me go, but his intent was no longer to hurt me. He started having pity on me, being himself an orphan.

He claimed that he was a real orphan having lost his mother in infancy. He would contend that having a mother disqualified me from being a true orphan.

He would explain it this way:

"You don't know how it is coming home to an empty house. I seldom find my father home except when he would intercept my school report and then it would be an occasion for a sound beating for my poor showing in the tests. I wish it was my father who had died instead of my mother. I tell you, a mother is more important for a kid than a father!"

I was too scared to challenge him on this point. Moreover, it gave me solace that not having a father spared me the pain and humiliation which he was subjected to by his father.

Over the next few years Mohamed Ali and I became friends and he assumed the role of my protector from the other bullies in the school. Sometimes he would share his candies with me. I would miss him when he was absent from school. He would explain his absences by just saying he was not well. On occasions I noticed black and blue marks on his body the cause of which he would not divulge. He did not like to talk about them and got angry when pressed. On several occasions he was called up to the Principal's office to be admonished for his absences and the poor academic record.

His father occasionally appeared at the Principal's office at the latter's behest. Mohamed Ali kept this aspect of his life a secret from me and the other classmates.

Gradually his absences became more frequent and the black and blue marks on his body more conspicuous. There were days when I would notice prominent bumps on his head and face.

He would dismiss these as a result of his falls during sports and fights with kids in his neighborhood. Then suddenly he stopped coming to school all together. I missed his company and lively mischievousness.

More than eighty years after the event, as I reflect on that unique and special friend of mine, I realize how he suffered and endured his misery in silence. Mohamed Ali was obviously a victim of child abuse. He did not relate this abuse even to me who was his close friend over the years.

Instinctively, the bully must have finally realized that I too was a victim. Perhaps he saw himself in me every time I flinched in anticipation of his punches. He must have related my meekness to his own inability to change a difficult situation. Mohamed Ali had no siblings, his mother had died during childbirth and he sought companionship with me. I was his foster family.

Through the story of Mohamed Ali I have learned how to appreciate another person's perspective in life. Mohamed Ali's position that you are not really an orphan unless you have lost your mother may not fit the dictionary description of "orphan," but through the filter of his mind and all that he had experienced, that definition made perfect sense. That definition of the word "orphan" provided him with a means to find pride in otherwise humiliating and abusive experience.

We are all villains to some degree, but fortunately, God can use even a villain to fulfill His master plan. It is good to befriend a victim; it is better to show empathy for a villain. When you see a villain say, "there but for the grace of God go I." Since all of us are both victim and villain, Jesus calls us to "love your enemy." This edict takes away the burden of revenge, and it bridges the inconsistency within our very own soul. Jesus further displays the perfect model of redemption and healing when he gives this simple command: "love one another." If you follow this command you may suddenly find that your enemy is your friend.

Within each and everyone of us there is both a victim and a villain. For example, as a victim, I never stopped complaining that my shoes hurt, not even when I met a man without feet; as a villain, I stole another man's shoes, or worse, I chopped off another man's feet. Your enemy's struggles are similar to your struggles; maybe, just maybe, your enemy is a greater victim then you, and you are a greater villain then he.

Originally authored by: Syed Abdullah, MD; Edited by: Ghazanfar Abdullah, MD, FAAC.

How I Expanded As I Shrank

I used to be a dedicated gardener. Flowers and vegetables adorned our garden. We also planted a variety of fruit trees: apples, almonds, quince, apricots, plums, peaches, pears and many more. There were a variety of cherries and berries, all very fruitful. We also built a small lean-to greenhouse which could be accessed from the living quarters. Looking back, it is amazing how much time and energy was spent on this hobby for about forty years.

And then, ten years ago, the decline set in. It became increasingly difficult for me to dig or to bend down to weed and plant. The first to go was the vegetable patch. Then the planting of ornamentals was curtailed. We had to hire somebody to maintain the lawn. My back hurt so much that my love for plants became confined mostly to the greenhouse.

After a period of despair, I discovered the exciting possibility of growing plants under the glass. I developed a fascination for starting seeds and watching them sprout and flourish. In the greenhouse I could also propagate plants from cuttings and by rooting. These activities could be carried on round the year and around the clock. One could walk into the greenhouse and commune with the plants anytime of the day or night. It is a joy to watch how the little seedlings respond to tender care. Within the confines of the greenhouse my love for plants developed a new, more intimate, dimension.

Reading books and collecting them in my personal library was another activity which I cherished all my life. Gradually every shelf and all the space in the office, basement, living room, dining room, bedroom, den and attic was filled with books bought at random and stored away as it was impossible to read them all. Finally I had to stop stockpiling books. I became more selective in what I read and often asked myself "Why am I reading this?" I also noted that spending long hours bent over books was producing eyestrain and worsening the backaches. Curtailing the obsessive habit of reading every book that came my way became a necessity. The same was true of the profusion of professional and lay magazines that came in the mail. By becoming more selective I eased the burden of having to plough through heaps of unwanted books and journals.

In the process of shrinking away from this compulsion I had more time to sit back, with eyes closed, and review all the years of random readings which were clogging my mind. Some of these I could not remember having ever read. There was a huge library tucked away somewhere in my consciousness waiting to be perused. These have been an inexhaustible source of pleasure and information emerging from within. To these were added memories of words of wisdom that I had picked up in the course of the years. These enriched and expanded my intellectual horizons as I saw faces of the kindly wise ones who had enhanced my perspective on life and invoked in me the love and caring for all.

My wife and I had another time-consuming and tiring hobby. We used to enjoy throwing lavish dinners for friends and relatives. We were acclaimed for these parties by all those who knew us. She is a great cook and went along with my expansive craving for having lots of company.

As we aged and became less capable of maintaining such a lifestyle, we started limiting these parties. Now we are content with having small intimate weekly get-togethers and enjoy them immensely. It gives us the opportunity to commune with friends without elaborate dinners to distract from the topics under discussion. Depending on the mood of the evening and the participants, we talk about poetry, literature and spiritual matters. My dear wife, who is aging along with me, does not have to spend that much time cooking. The quality of these modest affairs has improved our lives greatly. Here we test our ideas before going public with them. These are truly very creative and intellectually stimulating occasions.

Then, seven years ago, I joined the writing group with Eve. It has been a sheer joy to be in the company of such special people as Blanch, Bernadette, Barbara, Betty, Pearl, Peggy, Libby, Lillian, Justina, Joan, the Dorises, Jimmy, James, Harold, Elliot, Allan and the others. I remember with much fondness Jerry who passed away four years ago – a great guy who kept coming to the group despite his terminal illness.

Now in my nineties the process of shrinkage continues. There is still a lot of redundancy in my life which I am trying to get rid of to become unencumbered and free. People call me a psychiatrist, "a shrink". I seem to be doing just that----shrinking.

Essay by my father, Syed Abdullah, MD.

Preparing for eternity

Dear Papa,

Thank you Papa for giving us a glimpse of the life you and a Amma have lived! You may have lost the energy to do a lot of the things that you did in the past, but as a couple, your spirit and your love and harmony have never been stronger than it is today. Maybe that's just because you're both too weak to fight, or because you've learned to pick your battles carefully, almost avoiding them all. Your legacy will live on long after you both leave this earth. To those who know you both it is a privilege and an honor to serve you while you're still on this side of eternity! Heaven is waiting with open arms, but don't go yet!

Your loving son,
Ghazanfar.

God is love

Dear Ghazanfar,

God is Love" you said it last time you were here. I agree. God's love is the glue with which all creation is held together.

His love and mercy engulf the erring and the righteous ----the sun shines on all irrespectively. Anger veils us from His love so we cannot see clearly. But He sees us nevertheless.

Wealth and children are His gifts to us to cherish and be thankful for. They are also a test of our faith.

We give of our bounties to the next of kins, to the orphans, the needy, the wayfarer and to those who are burdened with obligations.

It is through giving with love, that we receive from His unlimited treasures.

Letter by
Syed Abdullah, MD.

The Sinner's Prayer.

Throughout the history of man people have tried to reach up to God, but in one instance God reached down to man, and that was when God sent Jesus in the flesh to the world, to be an exchange for our sins. Jesus was the sacrificial lamb whose righteousness we can partake of because he was slain at the cross of Calvary. Without that righteousness we would not be permitted by God to stand sinless and guiltless before Him. For this sacrifice I thank you Jesus.

Jesus, you are more than a brother to me, and you are more than my king. You did not have to leave the side of Father God, and the Holy Spirit, to come and save me, but you did so out of your love. There is no greater love than the one who gave his life for another, and you gave your life for a worm such as I. I am a sinner, desperately in need for a savior, and you are my savior.

Thank you for freely offering me salvation, not because of my works, but because of your work on the cross, your obedience to God the father. And thank you, Holy Spirit, for transforming my heart and guiding my way. Amen.

Elsayed: hey, wait a minute! That was a much better prayer than the one I recited in my heart when I became a Christian. Why didn't you read me that one instead of telling me to just wing it?

Abdullah: your personal prayer was fine. You don't have to be verbose to ask for Jesus to come into your life.

Elsayed: Tell me something about your mother. How did she raise you to be a Muslim in America?

Abdullah: She did not raise me to be a Fundamentalist Muslim. In America we thankfully have a watered down version of Islam. The last chapter of this book is a message to Muslims.

Chapter 9: Understanding Muslims.

What would Jesus do with Muslims? (WWJDWM).

Many times throughout history man has tried to reach up to God; but only once did God reach down to man, and this was through the person of Jesus Christ. Mohammed was not sent by God as an atoning sacrifice for my sin, but Jesus was. Unlike Muslims and Jews, who sacrifice goats and lambs for the atonement of sin, Jesus was the 'lamb of God,' he was slain for our the atonement of our sins. What friend is better than the one who is willing to lay down his life for us? Jesus gave us his all so that we have freedom from sin and we can enter paradise.

John 15:13 NIV

[13] Greater love has no one than this: to lay down one's life for one's friends.

History tells us that Jesus had a very unnatural way to fight a battle. He did not rely on the strength of his own arm, he did not have an army; he would pray for his enemies; he never lifted a finger to defend himself or his religion, and his weapon of choice was the wooden cross upon which he was crucified. The Christian Crusades were political battles fought by war mongers who, like the Muslim fundamentalist today, pretend to wage holy war for God's glory but really had other, mostly political motives. Jesus had no use for worldly gain through battles against fleshly enemies, he did not even hold his tormentors responsible, for he knew that the real battle was against Satan.

Ephesians 6:12 NIV

[12] For our struggle is not against flesh and blood, but against the rulers, against the authorities, against the powers of this dark world and against the spiritual forces of evil in the heavenly realms.

History tells us that Mohammed fought many battles to ensure the viability of Islam, his new religion. Mohammed was a prophet, a statesman, and a soldier. He was born through natural childbirth, and he never claimed to have any miraculous powers. In the Koran, Sura 17, verse 93, Mohammed describes himself to his disciples who were eager for him to show them a miracle: "Am I aught but a man----a messenger?" Mohammed did not perform miracles, he describes himself as a messenger, a man, and a sinner; in the Hadiths (sayings of Mohammed), it is written that Mohammed would repent for his sins seventy-two times each day. In Sura 19, verse 19, the Koran calls Jesus sinless, "A man without fault." And what else does the Koran say about Jesus? The Koran has an entire chapter dedicated to Jesus, which acknowledges the miracles of Jesus Christ, including his virgin birth, and his ability to breath life into a inanimate clay bird. Both the Koran and the Bible agree that Jesus performed miracles only by the power of God, and with God's permission.

As a child growing up in America, my Muslim mother taught me that you couldn't be a Muslim if you didn't believe in Jesus and his miracles. She said Jesus was *'the prophet of love'*; Moses who came before Jesus, was ' the prophet of the law'; and then there came Mohammed, who was *'the last prophet,'* through whom we could obtain *'the knowledge of God.'* The same monotheistic God sent all three prophets. My mother said it was irreverent against God's majesty to call Jesus 'the son of God.' She said that God is too high and mighty to have a family; but as a Christian I know the reason that God calls himself 'Father God,' is because He wants to adopt all of us as His 'lost children.' That is precisely what makes God so awesome to the Christian: the creator of the universe, my creator, desires a personal relationship with me, no mater how insignificant my life may be.

My mother also taught me that jihad was the unseen battle we fight every day, men and women, against Satan who seeks to control our minds and our hearts. That sounds remarkably similar to the battle that Christians fight when they "put on the armor of God "against Satan in spiritual warfare. Ephesians chapter 6. My mother taught me that the definition of the word 'Islam,' means "surrender to the will of God," but some other interpretations say that it is "surrender to the sword." Fundamentalist Muslims tend to agree with the latter definition.

So, in the famous words of Rodney King, "why can't we all just get along?" As a young Muslim growing up in America, a country full of Christians, that question really concerned me to the point that I had this dream:

I once dreamed that I was standing between two rails of a railroad track that stretched into the furthest horizon. A fire had broken out in front of me, and flames were consuming the rails. As I witnessed the rails gradually melt, I felt sad and hollow. I wanted to be on the train that used those tracks, but now my journey has ended because the flames had destroyed the tracks.

The two rails in my dream represented my dilemma: I was trying to decide between Christianity and Islam----the fire, Satanic fire---- was separating and destroying everything that should be together. Satan is our common enemy. Christians, Muslims, and even Jews, have more things in common than we have reasons to drift apart. Only by the love of God can we mend the tracks and get back on our journey. God is most interested in how we conduct ourselves during the journey. God does not care about our destination, as we do, because God is everywhere. Wherever we are, that is where God meets us and He showers us with love.

Christianity became irresistible to me because of the love of Jesus, the love of the Christians who ministered to me, and the love of God. No amount of legalism, or intellectual gymnastics could convince me to be **converted** to Christianity----I was never converted, but rather, I was **transformed** into being a Christian, a follower of Jesus, through the power of love. My heart and my internal circuitry were changed. If I were a computer, my old motherboard was removed, and it was replaced by a new one. But even so, you can not talk someone into understanding God's love; it must be through a transformed heart that a stubborn mind gets changed, not the other way around.

Therefore, the love of God is greater than the knowledge of God. Similarly, the sacrifice of Jesus neutralized the power that the Jewish law had. The Jewish law had only one purpose, and that was to confirm that no man was pious enough to make it to heaven on his own; we need the grace of God, and a savior to atone for our sins. The Bible says that "the ordinances of the law are nailed to the cross of Jesus Christ." ***Therefore, the knowledge of God, and the law of God, are both subservient to the love of God.*** That is why I am a Christian.

In my previous book, *Friends in Low Places*, I have a long chapter about giving apologetics to Muslims. Without becoming too verbose, I will end this section with **four simple points** on how to minister to Muslims:

- Ask if they believe that it is only through God's grace that we are saved, for in the Koran it is written that if we all got what we deserved than "Allah would not leave a single human being standing on the back of the earth." God chooses us to be saved----we don't deserve to be saved because of our works.

- Ask if they believe in the miracles of Jesus. The Koran has an entire chapter on Jesus----on his virgin birth, on how he breathed life into a clay-bird, etc. Adam and Eve created the original sin for all mankind. It is not so far-fetched for a Muslim to believe that Jesus could, by God's power, be resurrected from the dead and carry out God's plan for salvation of all mankind.

- Ask if they have ever seen Jesus in a dream or vision. There are many closet-Christians among the Muslim people. I was one.

- And most importantly, ask if you can pray with them! Prayer will melt your hearts together, and all boundaries between you will dissolve.

Don't have a Cow Man! Better Atone your Sins with the Blood of Jesus.

Muslims and Jews perform yearly animal sacrifices for the atonement of their sins; yet the inadequacy of last year's sacrifice is evident in the need for this year's sacrifice. In contrast, the blood of Jesus has ratified an eternal covenant with God, once and forever, and for all people, even those of us in the Bronx in the year 2021. By the blood of Jesus, the Lamb of God, our sins have been forgiven.

Hebrews 10:3-4 NIV

[3] But those sacrifices are an annual reminder of sins. [4] It is impossible for the blood of bulls and goats to take away sins.

Hebrews 10:19-20 NIV

[19] Therefore, brothers and sisters, since we have confidence to enter the Most Holy Place by the blood of Jesus, [20] by a new and living way opened for us through the curtain, that is, his body.

We have lost our First Love.

In the Bronx, and everywhere else, we have forgotten our first love; that is, our love for God. Despite having hundreds of relationships, thousands of acquaintances, and being the life of the party, we are lonesome to God. That is why 'love is in need of love today,' as the song by Stevie Wonder says. And because we have lost our love for God we have lost our light, and we have lost our lamp stand. If only we could bring love back to planet earth, perhaps Adam and Eve would think that they were back in the garden of Eden.

Revelation 2:4-5 NIV

[4] Yet I hold this against you: You have forsaken the love you had at first. [5] Consider how far you have fallen! Repent and do the things you did at first. If you do not repent, I will come to you and remove your lamp stand from its place.

When the Bible says "God is love," that does not mean that God is some gooey, mushy, weak emotion. It means that, from our perspective, we cannot understand God through our mind, or through our strength, or through any faculty other than our hearts. It is only through our hearts that we can come to know God, it is only through love. But our attention is so easily diverted from God. We get caught up seeking skinniness, or wealth, or fashion, or anything else but God. We fail even when we are seeking good things like human love, happiness, and family.

Whenever I am consumed by the things of this world, I say this simple prayer, "Oh Lord, let the light of your glory shine more and more brightly in my life, and let the light of the world grow dimmer and dimmer in your presence."

Matthew 6:33 NIV

[33] But seek first his kingdom and his righteousness, and all these things will be given to you as well.

Without love there is no power, no testimony, and Christianity is a hollow, meaningless experience.

1 Corinthians 13:1-8 NIV

[1] If I speak in the tongues of men or of angels, but do not have love, I am only a resounding gong or a clanging cymbal. [2] If I have the gift of prophecy and can fathom all mysteries and all knowledge, and if I have a faith that can move mountains, but do not have love, I am nothing. [3] If I give all I possess to the poor and give over my body to hardship that I may boast, but do not have love, I gain nothing. [4] Love is patient, love is kind. It does not envy, it does not boast, it is not proud. [5] It does not dishonor others, it is not self-seeking, it is not easily angered, it keeps no record of wrongs. [6] Love does not delight in evil but rejoices with the truth. [7] It always protects, always trusts, always hopes, always perseveres. [8] Love never fails.

God gently calls us, but the word of God is a double edged sword.

Religion says, "I will go and find God." Atheism says, "God does not exist, I am my own god." The believer says, "Not sure what I am feeling, but I have this strange attraction to the person of Jesus, and it's coming from the deepest recesses of my soul. I believe God has come to look for me!"

I always like to tell my crack-addict patients that I envy them. In disbelief, they ask, "What? Why?" But then I continue, saying, "Jesus loves all of his sheep, but your fat-cat doctor is like one of his ninety nine sheep in the safety of the pen; you, a crack-addict, are outside the pen. The crack addict is so lost that he is found. Not by his own doing but because God comes looking for you. I envy you because Jesus himself is coming to look for you!"

My biological son, aka Lil' gangster, Adam, asked me why I tend to use Biblical examples to solve worldly problems. My answer: the word of God is timeless and transferable. It is transferable from the individual to the society, from an affluent neighborhood to the Bronx, from generation to generation, and from era to era. The words of the Bible are as true today as they were thousands of years ago. That is why I use 'spiritual talk' to solve secular problems.

2 Timothy 3:16-17 NIV

[16] All Scripture is God-breathed and is useful for teaching, rebuking, correcting and training in righteousness, [17] so that the servant of God may be thoroughly equipped for every good work.

Yet, there is another reason to wield the word of God, and the name of Jesus, it is because Jesus is 'the name above all names,' and God's word is the sword that slays our eternal enemy, Satan. Beware that the word of God is a double edged sword----it also cuts the one who wields it. God has very little patience for those of us who are lukewarm seekers. God wants us to passionately seek him, and He holds pastors and leaders of the church to an even higher standard than the rest of us.

Revelation 12:11 NIV[11]

They triumphed over him by the blood of the Lamb and by the word of their testimony; they did not love their lives so much as to shrink from death.

Chapter 10: Ten texts, Difficult Questions, Life Changing Answers.

Excerpts from the book: Great Men and Praying Women

Ghazanfar Abdullah:

Adam Elsayed:

Elsayed: What makes a good wife? How do I know if I found the right person?

Abdullah: In answer to your question, you don't "find" the right person, instead, you become the right person, and as a couple you become the right people. The Bible says, after marriage a man and a woman become "one flesh." What started as two individuals becomes one couple.

Marriage is medicine for loneliness. The right Medicine, at the right dose, can cure your blues; but too much of even the right medicine can be poisonous; and even a small amount of the wrong medicine will kill you fast.

Having common goals in life is actually more important than being in love. This is because no one really knows what love is when we are young and foolish, but it is easier to quantify the goals that will keep us moving in the right direction as husband and wife. The greatest goal, of course, is to seek first the kingdom of God as a couple. The Bible says if you seek God first then he will grant you all that you need in your life.

And finally, there is the 'risk versus benefit' analysis. My girlfriend, who later became my wife, asked, "are we ever going to get married one day?" To which I answered, "if the reasons for us to stay together outweigh the reasons for us to move apart, then we will definitely stay together and be married."

Overtime, it hurt too much to leave her, and it felt just right to stay. Love was beginning to gel in our lives. There were more reasons to stay, more common goals, and the best goal was to serve God together for life. And so we got married in three months after I met her. My friends and my family said we were crazy. My oldest son, Adam, helped us make the decision to get married long before he was even born. It seems that Adam was conceived in a little town, just outside of wedlock! Neither of us believed in abortion. So, as much of a pain in the ass my son Adam has turned out to be, he was and still is, the glue that holds our family together!

The turning point for me was when I found out just how much my girlfriend loved God. Whenever she talked about God she would have tears in her eyes from a strong spiritual desire to love Him. I fell in love with a woman who loved God more than she loved her own life, and more than she loved me. I knew the ride would be bumpy because we were not of the same religion, but the most important thing was our shared goal to seek God, and to love God.

I convinced her to Convert to Islam, which she did for the first 10 years of our marriage, followed by converting back to born-again Christianity at year 10, followed by my conversion to born- again Christianity, by year 14 of our marriage. It was a rocky ride between year 10 and year 14, to say the least! 35 years later, the rocks on the road of our marriage have become smaller, and smaller, and now they are just pebbles by the grace of God. After all these years I have the authority to tell her to "cut it out," whenever she stresses the small stuff (the pebbles). Sometimes I take the batteries out of my hearing aids.

God honors our little house because we honor his grand kingdom. Joseph said, in the Bible, "as for me and my house, we will serve the Lord."

Elsayed: What if my wife doesn't want to crawl into my chest cavity, like in your poem? Can I have buyers remorse? Can I get a divorce? So, if my future wife, God forbid, can't have any children for some reason, and procreation is the main reason for sex, is that grounds for divorce?

Abdullah: No, you can't divorce your wife just because she can't get pregnant. Jesus said that adultery is the only reason for divorce, because the marriage commitment/covenant was desecrated. There is no easy way out of marriage once you have entered the marriage covenant. Husbands and wives must show grace, mercy and forgiveness toward one another. God is not in favor of division, but rather He wants unity despite hard circumstances.

The Bible is full of stories of barren women being able to give birth after the couple started to pray for the miracle of pregnancy. Abraham and Sarah were 100 years old when they had their first child, and Abraham is known as "the father of all nations."

Procreation isn't the main reason for sex. Sex is also a celebration of being one flesh with your spouse. You are celebrating an intimate relationship with one other person, in a manner that mirrors our unique relationship with God.

Sex is an act of worship, and children are a blessing from God, but there needs to be a commitment to stay together and raise a family.

Timing a family is difficult. The best time for a woman to give birth, from a physiological perspective, is between the ages of 20 and 30; on the other hand, men can procreate as long as they have a sufficient sperm count, and these soldiers know how to swim straight.

Not everyone wants to have a family, nor should everyone have a family. An elderly man shouldn't have children if he cannot spend time raising them because he is too weak and feeble. If a 30 year old woman gives birth to a female child, that puts her future menopause in alignment with her daughter's future premenstrual syndrome——there will be lots of fights and big trouble in twenty years.

The best time to have a marriage and start a family is when you're too young and stupid to realize what you're getting into. That's probably in your mid 20s, for a woman, and in your mid 30s for a man. Men stay stupid longer. Once you start having a family you need to pray a lot for God's help, because life just got a whole lot more complicated. That's why it is important to finish school, get a job, and be a 'go getter' before having children, because children rightly will occupy much of your time and effort.

Above all, don't be a polygamist, because this grieves God. Your Muslim father was a polygamist, but every married man who views pornography is also a polygamist. The lewd images on a computer screen take away time, energy, and trust from his wife and family. It's hard enough for a married couple to stay together, the forces of evil are all around, but sex between a husband and a wife is God's glue to help keep us together. That glue cannot be shared with anyone outside of the marriage, and definitely not wasted on Internet pornography. "Oh, but my wife's mean to me when she's having her period, so I go on the Internet and look at porn."

Don't do porn! If your wife is cruel to you, do this: suck it up, and keep it moving. Find a way to make your wife smile again. Spend your time, energy, and prayers in an effort to build up your family life. Real men don't require Vaseline. They require duct tape, gorilla glue, and 10W40. Real men fix things, they glue the broken pieces, and they take away rust from the past, and keep it moving.

The broken pieces may be from her childhood trauma, you must gather the pieces and apply duct tape and gorilla glue. Her innocent childhood emotions may have gathered rust from years of anxiety, depression, and mistrust——nothing that a little 10W40 can't fix. A little anointing oil can return her to smooth innocence. A good man knows how to troubleshoot his family, his wife, and himself, and he keeps it moving. Moving toward the kingdom of God.

Elsayed: "treat others as they would want to be treated----not necessarily the way you want to be treated." I never heard this saying. I absolutely love it.

Abdullah: That's called 'the platinum rule of marriage,' as opposed to Jesus's 'golden rule,' which is to "do unto others as you would have them do unto you." Why the upgrade? It is because we are to treat our wives better than we would treat anyone else in the world. The pedestal we make for our wives is very high, and it is very heavy, so she can't pick it up and throw it at you when she's mad.

Elsayed: Is the Holy Spirit God Himself?

Is He a separate entity? Or are Him, God, and Jesus one in the same?

Abdullah: The short answer——I am one person, yet I have a first, last, and a middle name; another example, the sun is one entity, yet it has light, mass, and heat. Hence, the Holy Spirit, God, and Jesus are three perspectives of the same being, which we call the Holy Trinity.

The identity of Jesus I will address elsewhere, but let us focus on the person of the Holy Spirit, and let's answer the age old question, "who is God, and how can we know him?"

Our perception of things depends on us using the appropriate corresponding sense. How do we perceive love? Not by our five senses. Mountains of poetry, and millions of love songs, cannot explain what love is. The reason why the Bible says "God is love," Is to remind us that we cannot use any of our five senses to perceive his presence; it is only through our hearts that we can feel that God's love is near. Love is God's language, and the organ of perception is the human heart. We cannot manipulate God to get to know him, but God can be loved, and He reveals himself to those with a pure, childlike heart.

The Holy Spirit is like a fragrance that is carried by the wind. You can't see the wind but you know it's there because of the action that it takes when it blows a sailboat across the sea, or blows the hat off of a person who was walking down the street. Similarly, you can't see a fragrance, but anyone who goes into the bathroom after I've been in it will know that I was there! I left my fragrance behind. I don't want to sound blasphemous, but we know God was here because of His fragrance, the Holy Spirit, was left behind. And look, he left the seat up again!

——the seat joke pertains to me, not God! No blasphemy here.

I heard someone once say, "Jesus is my plunger, who keeps it moving, when sin clogs my pipes." Ok, that's blasphemous, but I heard that from a janitor friend who had just come to know the Lord, and he had us all rolling in laughter when he said, "Jesus is my plunger," at a men's retreat.

Do you remember, in your earliest childhood memories, how your grandmother smelled? I am 60 years old now and I can still remember how my grandmother used to smell, from my earliest memories before the age of three. When I go to heaven, and find my grandmother there, I will feel her love because that fragrance will be apparent, long before I ever see her with my eyes. The Holy Spirit is like that fragrance, it is the fragrance of love. It is the fragrance of someone you love, and it gives you comfort beyond your understanding.

I have five granddaughters and one grandson. Whenever Aubrey, my oldest granddaughter, hears me singing Christian hymns, in my deep baritone voice, she comes running to me, shouting, "grandpa is in the Spirit! Grandpa is in the Spirit!" She knows, at her tender age, that the Holy Spirit is near when grandpa bellows out a "God song."

How does my seven-year-old granddaughter know that I am "in the Spirit?" It is because she has developed her heart to know the things of God. Here is an essay about a grandson who smells the fragrance of his grandfather and finds peace. It is called, "his grandpa's shirt."

Elsayed: Why are we here? What's our purpose? Is it because God condemned Adam?

Abdullah: The short answer is that our sole purpose is to glorify God. That is our only purpose. We are to glorify God, utilizing our free will; unlike the angels, who also glorify God, but do so robotically, because they have no free will outside of God's will.

Our free will makes it possible to rise above the angels, but it can also make us sink below the animals, if we misuse it. Animals have instinct, they kill to eat; but humans, with our free will, kill for sport; and angels only kill if it is God's will.

Adam and Eve had their chance to stay in paradise and enjoy a perfect relationship with God. However, sin intervened and God had to separate himself from his human creation. Jesus felt this separation, due to the sin of all humanity, when he was on the cross and asked God "why have you forsaken me?"

The worst thing that can happen to a human being is separation from God, and the best thing that can happen to a human being is reconciliation with God. Jesus made a path for us to be reconciled with God despite our sin.

Elsayed: How do you know you've found a good mentor? Where do you look for one?

Abdullah: God sends people into your life, as long as you are a seeker of God. For example, if God hadn't sent me into your life, then he would've sent someone else. The bottom line is that you were a seeker of God. Just be you. Stay thirsty for God. The seeker never finds God, but God finds the seeker. It's like the story of the little boy who was lost in the mall. When the police finally reunited him with his mother he told the police, "my mommy was lost, it's a good thing you helped me find her."

You take one step towards God, and He takes 100 steps towards you. It's like the parable of the one lost sheep. God comes looking for the one sheep that is lost, leaving the 99 sheep that are safely found. God is actively drawing us nearer to Him: the more you are lost, the more you are seeking God, the more He will pull you closer to Him.

If you thirst for God, then he will thirst for you. As an old Islamic proverb says, "oh you who are thirsty for the tea, you don't realize that the tea is also thirsty for you."

If you pray for guidance, and keep a pure heart and an open mind, then God will send you the right mentor. This will be in addition to your internal mentor, which is the Holy Spirit, who dwells in every believer's heart.

Elsayed: How do you stay motivated? What sort of goals should I be setting for myself? Strictly monetary based for now while establishing my career? I know you said when you have faith God provides for you but it seems like you were ambitious even before your strong connection with Him.

Abdullah: Are you are aware that most people don't fully utilize the Holy Spirit power that lives in our hearts; are you aware that we only use about 2% of our brains? How do we maximize the power of our hearts and our brains?

The Bible has the answer. Simply put, worship God and think of beautiful things. Some people think that spirituality is a big waste of time, but the greatest epiphanies in my life have come while I was seeking God with all of my heart, mind, and strength. If I didn't worship God and think of beautiful things, instead, I would worship my own foolish ambitions and dwell on negative thoughts. In short, I would become a slave of Satan. What is the rat race? It is a bunch of negative people, who worship their own progress, while never thinking to advance the kingdom of God. The opposite of this is when we follow the scripture that says, "seek first the kingdom of God, and His righteousness, and all of these things will be added onto you."

You can chew gum and walk at the same time. You can seek God, worship him, and think of beautiful things, even while you pursue your education, advancement at your job, and a family life. The two are not mutually exclusive. God wants you to prosper in this life, and also in the life here after. Worldly success is linked to our spiritual success. I will give you an example.

Remember, I told you that God sometimes comes to us in dreams and visions. I often wakeup at three or four o'clock in the morning with an answer to one of my burning questions. For instance, during the early days of the HIV epidemic, I once woke up with a dream of a spider's web. I instantly knew, in my heart and in my brain, that God was telling me to combine Ritonivir with other protease inhibitors to get a boosting effect that would help me treat my HIV patients, and to prevent them from dying. When I attended an HIV conference that was held by the makers of Ritonivir, Abbott laboratories, I looked like a genius. I was everyone's hero when I stated that I combined this medication with other protease inhibitors and achieved startling good results.

God's wisdom, not my own, was revealed to me through a dream. It might've taken me 30 years to get to that point without God's help. I have an unfair advantage over other researchers in the field of HIV. And my clinic has a success rate of over 90%, which is unheard of in the South Bronx. To God be the glory if my patients do well, to me be the reason if they do poorly. I'm just a man, I make mistakes, but God is the master physician.

Finally, worshiping God and focusing on all that is beautiful in life, makes life much more fun. I love to marvel at the trees, the streams, the animals, the insects, and all that God has created. God has a sense of humor, and Jesus must've known every stupid idea that was going through his disciples heads, as they were thinking, but the joke's on us. God wants us to live a fully joyful, productive life on earth, followed by a total worship party, forever and ever, in heaven.

What could be better than that?

Elsayed: Is there a judgement day for Christians as well? How do Christians repent after they've sinned and already became baptized?

Abdullah: Yes, Christians believe in the day of judgment. But I think the question you're really asking is, do Christians believe that Salvation gives them a license to live in sin? Although, our salvation does not depend on our deeds, the Christian will not sin because he fears that it will grieve God. Again, think of the child and his father. If a child loves his father then he will not want to grieve his father; he will do what his father says simply because he wants to hear the words, "well done my good and faithful servant." Those are the words that God will speak to us when we stand at the threshold of heaven. The following scripture is an account, in the words of Jesus himself, of the day of judgment:

Luke 21:25-36 NIV

[25] "There will be signs in the sun, moon and stars. On the earth, nations will be in anguish and perplexity at the roaring and tossing of the sea. [26] People will faint from terror, apprehensive of what is coming on the world, for the heavenly bodies will be shaken. [27] At that time they will see the Son of Man coming in a cloud with power and great glory. [28] When these things begin to take place, stand up and lift up your heads, because your redemption is drawing near." [29] He told them this parable: "Look at the fig tree and all the trees. [30] When they sprout leaves, you can see for yourselves and know that summer is near. [31] Even so, when you see these things happening, you know that the kingdom of God is near. [32] "Truly I tell you, this generation will certainly not pass away until all these things have happened. [33] Heaven and earth will pass away, but my words will never pass away. [34] "Be careful, or your hearts will be weighed down with carousing, drunkenness and the anxieties of life, and that day will close on you suddenly like a trap. [35] For it will come on all those who live on the face of the whole earth. [36] Be always on the watch, and pray that you may be able to escape all that is about to happen, and that you may be able to stand before the Son of Man."

Abdullah: Muslims go to Mecca for pilgrimage and the atonement of their sins, They also sacrifice goats and lambs for the atonement of their sins. I have never been to Mecca in my lifetime, and since becoming a Christian, I have stopped sacrificing animals to shed their blood for my sin. What have I replaced Mecca and the blood of animals with? How are my sins atoned?

As a Christian, I don't have to go anywhere, because wherever I am, God is here. My heart is the temple of the Holy Spirit. I have the word of God in my Bible, I have the blood of Jesus that was spilled for me and all sinners, once and for all, for everyone who was ever created by God Almighty. I don't sacrifice bovine animals, but I do occasionally enjoy a cheeseburger at McDonald's.

During the pandemic my pastor said to us that, even if the church is closed physically, it does not mean that it is closed spiritually. This is because every believers heart is the church. Our hearts are the temple of the Holy Spirit of God. We cannot be separated from the Love of God, because God lives in us, and he does His miraculous work through us.

Elsayed: Why do Christians make so much noise during praise and worship? It can get a little annoying.

Abdullah: Praise and Worship will Break Every Chain. Praise and worship turns us away from a life of self-determination, as we start to depend on God. When we rely on the love of the Creator we build confidence, as a child who calls out loud to his benevolent father.

Matthew 7:9-11 NIV [9] "Which of you, if your son asks for bread, will give him a stone? Or if he asks for a fish, will give him a snake? [11] If you, then, though you are evil, know how to give good gifts to your children, how much more will your Father in heaven give good gifts to those who ask him!"

I remember my first experience with Christian praise and worship came while I was visiting my wife's church. I was confused. As a Muslim, I found it irreverent that the Christians used a five piece band to help them pray to God. What was this place, a concert hall, or a place of worship? Never having heard these songs, I would quietly read the words that were projected on the screen. While still a Muslim, I was intensely moved by the worship songs that the Christians would sing. I was hardly moving my lips to the song when I heard a soft still voice inside my head say, "even though no one can hear you sing, I hear you. I hear the song in your heart, and I love the way that you sing." For the first time in my wife's church, a tear came to my eye.

God has a sense of humor. Several years later I was moved to join the worship team. I was one of only four singers, and yes we had a five piece band: my son Adam played the saxophone, and my son Raza played the drums. I sang baritone, like the Pakistani Barry White that I always wanted to be. I would sing to God, in a deep voice, "I can't get enough of your love."

I needed to learn how to praise and worship before God could use me to advance his Kingdom. I needed a 'jail-break' for my singing voice before God permitted me to use my pen.

Elsayed: Christians seem to always have more fun than Muslims and Jews. And then there's bacon, so delicious. But seriously, with so many deep conflicts happening around the world, (Palestinian Israeli conflict and Afghanistan), and if God is a part of our family, why does He allow so many bad things to happen to so many people?

Abdullah: Although most Muslims are peaceful, a fanatical few have interpreted the language of the Koran as a command to kill the 'kafirs,' usually Christians and Jews (kafir means infidel or unbeliever, or someone who does not believe in one God and the day of judgment). The terrorist's war against Christians and Jews is misguided even by the standard set by the Koran. This is because Christians and Jews are not atheists or polytheists; they do believe in 'one God and the day of judgment'----there is no reason for Muslims to kill Christians and Jews on theological grounds, they are not kafirs. The Koran says that if you meet a Christian or a Jew "you should try to outdo one another in good deeds," it does not say "behead them." The Koran calls Christians and Jews "the people of the book," worthy of partnership, theological discussions, and spiritual exploration.

What is the history of radical, Islamic terrorism? War between rival Arab tribes was a fact of life during early Islam, and this is reflected in the writings of the Koran. For thousands of years the Middle East has been a cesspool for wars between Arab tribes, it would be wise for our politicians not to pick sides. In modern times, the Muslim's theological battle against non-Muslim Arab tribes have been replaced by a battle against Christians and Jews. Christians and Jews provide the usual target for a holy war, or jihad; but other Muslim 'tribes' have served as targets, particularly if they do not believe in the exact same version of Islam, as does the jihadist. These violent scriptures of the Koran are not transferable to modern times:

Sura 33, vs 61: they shall have a curse on them, and wherever they are found, they shall be seized and slain without mercy.

Sura 9, vs 29: slay those who believe in neither Allah or the last day.

Sura 22, vs 39: to those against whole war is made, permission is given to slay, because they are wrong and verily Allah is most powerful for your aid.

So why does God permit radical, Islamic terrorism? I would like to give a Christian overview of why God permits all suffering, and even terrorism. Here are three points: first, God honors the free will of man, including the terrorists will to bring death and distraction. Atheists will say that terrorism proves that God does not exist. A 'good God' would not have permitted terrorism if God really existed. Which leads me to my second point, God permitted terrorism to draw Believers to seek Him----persecution strengthens the church. Christianity in America has never been confronted with persecution until now. Third point: in the end God always wins. Now let's expand on these three points.

The apostle Paul writes, in **2Corinthians 12:10**, "that is why, for Christ's sake, I delight in weaknesses, and insults, and hardships, in persecutions, and difficulties. For when I am weak, then I am strong, because God's power is made perfect in weakness. " Ask any persecuted Christian missionary serving around the world, and he will say, "in the moment of our greatest suffering, we develop clarity to our vision so that we can plainly see God." Strangely, it seems that God is closest to us when we are in despair, and with our backs up against a wall.

Sometimes we even have to suffer at the hands of mortals to feel the fullness of God's presence: ***with great burden comes greater love***. Survivors of 9/11 saw visions of Jesus in the stairwell; and as a sign of his presence, there was the amazing steel girders fashioned into a cross by the intense heat from the fire. God's love never forsakes us.

In the end God always wins. God has allowed Satan to have temporary dominion over the earth. Revelation 12:12 proclaims, "woe to the earth and sea, because the devil has gone down to you! He is filled with fury, because he knows that his time is short." Terrorists have prostituted themselves to Satan, but rest assured, God can take the most horrific deeds spawned by Satan, turn it upside down, and use it to destroy the forces of evil from within. God uses evil to cannibalize evil. The very people opposed to God are used as tools to execute God's will.

Revelation 17:8-17 says, "the beast and the 10 horns you saw will hate the prostitute; they will bring her to ruin and leave her naked; they will eat her flash and burn her with fire. For God has put it into their hearts to accomplish His purpose by agreeing to give the beast their power to rule, until God's words are fulfilled. "

There is solidarity with those who are suffering----I was once just a Muslim from Pakistan, but after 9/11, I have become a Christian from Manhattan Island. I could also relate with women and girls who suffer in Afghanistan under the Taliban rule.

I pray that God will invert the original purpose of these Satanic terrorist attacks, and as such, God will bring more people to become seekers of His love. When times are good, we Americans think that our success comes from our own wisdom and might. Persecution reminds us that we are still vulnerable and need to turn to God for protection and answers. Furthermore, we need to pray for those who persecute us, just as Jesus prayed for his tormentors when he was on the cross. Despite 9/11, if we are motivated to pray and practice fasting, America can regain her spiritual center of gravity, and many more Muslims can encounter the precious love of Jesus Christ. Amen.

Biography:

Coming from a Muslim background, my instinct was to steamroller my wife, and hate a Jew. But my wife wasn't having any of it. Women give good advice, and it often balances the arrogant, testosterone driven goals that we men tend to set for ourselves. My wife was hard to deal with, but I loved, honored, and respected her, and she helped me grow in every aspect of my life. The best advice for the Taliban is that they should love their wives the way Jesus loved the church, and he died for the church.

Adam Elsayed is a 27 year old, successful pharmaceutical representative who calls on my office. His father, a Muslim, left his family to start another family, when Adam was only 10 years old. Adam came to know about his father's parallel family only about a year before I met him. "Not cool," Adam opined. I could feel his pain, but in a strange sense we needed each other: he needed a father figure, and I needed to grow my spiritual family.

This book represents a running text conversation which culminates in Adam excepting Jesus Christ as his Savior. Now it is confirmed that spiritual bonds are stronger than biological roots. 22 years ago, when I first became a Christian, I cried out to the Lord for reconciliation with my Muslim relatives. In a moment of extreme clarity, I heard a soft, still voice say, "I am your family! And your sisters and brothers in the church are your real sisters and brothers. They are also your family."

Printed by Libri Plureos GmbH in Hamburg, Germany